WOMEN IN WHITE

The Haunting of Northeast Florida

Elizabeth Randall

Photographs by Bob Randall

Schiffer Publishing Ltd

4880 Lower Valley Road • Atglen, PA 19310

Published by Schiffer Publishing, Ltd.
4880 Lower Valley Road
Atglen, PA 19310
Phone: (610) 593-1777; Fax: (610) 593-2002
E-mail: Info@schifferbooks.com

For our complete selection of fine books on this and related subjects, please visit our website at www.schifferbooks.com.
You may also write for a free catalog.

This book may be purchased from the publisher.
Please try your bookstore first.

We are always looking for people to write books on new and related subjects. If you have an idea for a book, please contact us at proposals@schifferbooks.com.

Schiffer Publishing's titles are available at special discounts for bulk purchases for sales promotions or premiums. Special editions, including personalized covers, corporate imprints, and excerpts can be created in large quantities for special needs.
For more information, contact the publisher.

Library of Congress Control Number: 2015942760

Designed by RoS
Type set in BellCent BdList BT/Arrus BT

ISBN: 978-0-7643-4882-2
Printed in The United States

Praise for *Women in White*

Liz Randall has crafted a wonderfully offbeat narrative that describes in colorful detail a slice of Florida you won't find in the guide books. Randall helps us more fully appreciate how a supernatural world of eerie lights and scary noises and wispy apparitions of "Women in White" are a lot more a part of the Florida character than we may realize. If you think alligators in swimming pools and giant exotic snakes are strange, you ain't see nothing yet!

—Bill Belleville
Award-winning film maker and
Author of *Salvaging the Real Florida*

Author Elizabeth Randall suggests that history is somewhat fearful when it comes to capturing romance. "Women in White" know no such fear. You will find history and romance nicely intermixed. And, after all, isn't romance the stuff history is made of? A fun read!

—Major James Douglass Robertson
American humorist and author of *Robby*

Liz and Bob live on a secluded street in Lake Mary, Florida. Both are transplants from the North, but grew up in South and Central Florida. Liz is a long time writer, and Bob is making it a family thing. We all love ghost stories and this one is enough to turn you white.

— Richard Arthur King III
Historian, SAR, and Genealogist

The most current book by Bob and Elizabeth Randall, *Women in White: The Haunting of Northeast Florida*, presents a unique view of Florida history by imparting historical facts through the eyes of spirits. The writing appeals to all the senses enabling the reader to see, smell, and experience Florida history in a unique and enchanting way. This delightful twist of perspective enhances the reader's enjoyment of the Florida of the past. Anyone interested in history, the paranormal, or just a good story will love this book.

—Kris Lodrick
Educator in a top-ranking school district

Dedication

For Clara Randall
who loved history and whose spirit will
always remain an integral and beloved
presence within our own.

Epigram

"The smallest human interest that the pure heart can feel is appointed to immortality."

—Wilkie Collins
The Woman in White

CONTENTS

PREFACE

Bob and I are as close to being native Floridians as two interlopers from Maine and New York can be. We like to think we've evolved, from the settled suburbanites that we look like, into something deeper and more incongruous—something like explorers and adventurers of a northeast Florida state of mind.

We, who grew up amid autumn leaves falling like confetti, wading through waist-deep snowdrifts, wearing long sleeves on summer nights, now live with a gradation of seasons. It is a gradual shifting, a metamorphosis distinguishable only by the scent of flowers or the stink of fish guts, the intensity of a sunset, or the sighting of wild animals, amphibious or terrain reptiles, ambling along their ancient paths as they will continue to do when humans are long gone.

Long gone is the subject of this book. Some people would call our subject matter history and there is nothing wrong with that. However, history doesn't capture the romance, anguish, sacrifice, and grit of the northeastern Floridians who settled a section of a state so startling in its beauty and in its ruthlessness. The seasons may be subtle, but there is nothing temperate about the weather, the disposition, and the landscape that surrounds and ultimately inhabits the settlers and the seekers of northeast Florida.

In northeast Florida, sunsets spread across the sky like bloodstains, dissolving into the horizon, yielding nights where clouds stream across the face of the moon like ragged sheets. Eating the stem of native hibiscus is poison. Coral snakes, scorpions, bears, coyotes, gators, wild boars, wild turkeys, buzzards are still...everywhere. They survive the hurricanes, twisters, and sinkholes. Only the hardiest Floridians can claim the same.

These hardy northeastern Floridians, and the land they lived on, is the subject of *Women in White*. From the Timacuan Indians whose grave sites are found in gated suburban communities, to the nineteenth governor of Florida, Napoleon Bonaparte Broward, whose goal was to drain and to develop the Everglades, to the wretched criminals incarcerated in the blood-soaked Clay County jail, voices from northeast Florida's past echo and reverberate.

Bob and I didn't research the paranormal history of northeast Florida; we researched its history, and the paranormal is as much a part of its past as the yellowed clippings from *The Times-Union*. Ghost stories have been labeled, for far too long, as beneath the intellectual integrity of proven history. Nothing could be further from the truth. Ghosts are a metaphor for memory. Narrative is the way people understand their world. Combine the two, and the reality of the past becomes transparent, albeit intangible.

Although Bob and I have never seen a ghost, although we are not sure there are ghosts (we call ourselves "ghost agnostics") we have experienced a few "irregularities" during our visits to haunted historic sites for which there is no ready explanation. Actually, there were three incidents.

The first unexplained event occurred at The Book Loft, which is located in the historic district of Fernandina Beach in Nassau County. Bob was taking a picture and, out of nowhere, a glowing orb of light appeared. He snapped the picture, looked again, and it was gone. You can see the picture in Chapter 16.

The second unexplained event occurred at the New Berlin cemetery in Duval County. The day before our visit, I had spent some time at the Museum of Southern History. I met Lester A. Hardee, grandson of former governor Napoleon Bonaparte Broward. Lester spent some time telling me about the former statesman, including the fact that his first wife died within a year or two of their marriage, and his infant son a few months later. No one knew where the graves were. The following day, I stumbled across an old cemetery across the street from Yellow Bluff Fort. The first gravestone I laid eyes on in the New Berlin Cemetery marked the final resting place of the departed Mrs. Broward and her infant son: Napoleon Bonaparte Broward II. You can read the whole story in Chapter 7.

The last event occurred at the Clay County jail in Green Cove Springs. In picturesque Green Cove Springs, the St. Johns River widens, reflecting the overhanging greenery with mirror-like precision. It has a warm mineral spring gushing into a public swimming pool in the center of town and a whitewashed 100-year-old jail on the corner of Orange Avenue. The parking lot of the jail is where the heels of strangled prisoners dangled from the gallows they helped to construct.

The docent gave us a tour of the deserted jail, leading us up the rusty steps to the corridor where the most violent prisoners were kept. As I followed her down the walkway, taking notes, I heard a strange sound. To find out what it was read Chapter 2.

Many sincere and honest people who Bob and I interviewed claimed to have seen ghosts, apparitions, unexplained mist, and always a Woman in White. In fact, a northeast Florida State of Mind is dominated by wispy trails of Women in White. Researchers of paranormal folklore are bound to unearth stories of these translucent ladies; they constitute narratives throughout the world. There is no ready explanation for their appearance in ghost tales in every time zone, in every corner and pocket of humanity, in every book of ghost stories ever written.

Women in White stand and stare, they float, or they appear in mirrors, their tattered garments a mere memory of clothes, but always, always as white as the clouds, which they, earthbound as their souls remain, cannot hope to rise above. In this book, the Women White sightings appear in The Kingsley Plantation Chapter 5, and in The Homestead Restaurant, Chapter 9.

Bob and I sometimes wonder if we would have written this book if we had grown up in Florida, grown up accustomed to this huge green peninsula, instead of where we lived—facing the harsh realities of a northern and a New England winter. La Florida, land of flowers, has always been the more attractive research subject. Yet beneath the surface of northeast Florida's beauty, there is bloodshed, bodies, war, peace, courage, betrayal, heroism, brilliance, and just plain stupidity.

In fact, most of Florida's history is harder to believe than its ghost stories.

ACKNOWLEDGMENTS

We would like to thank Gail Wadsworth, Flagler County's Clerk of the Court, volunteer docents of Clay County Visitra R. Garig and Claude Bass, former resident of Franklintown, George Green, Teen Peterson, Collections Manager at the Amelia Island Museum of History and docents Steve and Penny Sansbury, Sterling Joyce maitre d' of the Casa Marina Hotel, and volunteer Lester A. Hardee of the Museum of Southern History.

As always, our thanks goes to author and mentor Bill Belleville, and to the last true Floridian, our good friend, Jack Bass.

Last, we can't fail to mention our daughter Courtney Randall, our granddaughter Cassidy Jasmann, and our daughter in spirit, Miranda LaGarde for giving us the motivation to get out of the house, to go exploring, and to leave them in charge.

INTRODUCTION

The ghost stories and the history of northeast Florida stem from some of its oldest counties. This includes Baker County, where the only Civil War battle ever fought in Florida took place in the bitter cold of a pine forest a few miles from its rallying point of Ocean Pond. Clay County was home to moonshine, turpentine, and the US military. Flagler County is an abridged remnant of St. Johns and Volusia counties.

In Duval County, the largest city in the state of Florida began as a county seat called "Cowford," although it was eventually renamed Jacksonville in honor of President Andrew Jackson. Periodically decimated by raging fires and yellow fever epidemics, the city continued its relentless growth in spite of all obstacles. Occupied by Union forces in a bitterly divided state during the Civil War, it was later used as a port for Cuban gunrunners and a set for silent films, helped by Hollywood money in the early twentieth century.

In Nassau County, which occupies the largest portion of the book, Amelia Island's history is long and exponentially complicated; in fact, it was, like all of northeast Florida, occupied long before European adventurers set it within their sights. Two thousand years ago, Timacuan Indians settled and thrived there. The Timacuan warrior tribe was heavily tattooed and wore clattering shells around their waists to alarm enemies. Primarily, however, it was a matriarchal society run by female chiefs. They lived in little round houses like the pre-Anglo-Saxons and drank "cassina," a caffeine-rich tea. They were happy and healthy before the Europeans arrived.

But arrive they did—to fight, squabble, murder, to hoist and to yank down flag after national flag. Even the names of Nassau County reflect the nationalistic merging of two separate countries. Named "Amelia" Island after an English princess, it is the last inhabited barrier island off the East Coast of the southern United States. Only thirteen miles long, and four miles wide, the island has one town, Fernandina Beach, named after Ferdinand II, a Spanish king.

Eight flags have flown over the island and the first, thanks to the devout Huguenot General Jean Ribault, was the French flag. But it was all downhill for France from there.

That would be around the sixteenth century, when the French Huguenots decided they needed a presence in the new world. Jean Ribault stepped ashore on the tip of the island very close to where, 450 years later, the fictional "Villa Villekulla" house used in the Pippi Longstocking movies was filmed. He became the first documented European visitor on Amelia Island soil. General Pedro Menendez de Aviles of Spain was under strict military orders to stop General Ribault, who had the bad luck to sail into an August hurricane and shipwreck his entire crew. The Spanish general managed to pick the French sailors off around the Matanza Inlet, executing the entire crew, which numbered in the hundreds, including Ribault.

The Spanish flag flew until 1763, when the Treaty of Paris ceded Florida to Britain in exchange for Havana, Cuba. Lord Egmont, an Englishman, bought a 10,000-acre estate covering almost the entire terrain of Amelia Island. At one time, he toyed with the idea of naming the barrier island "Egmont Isle." He also brought the plantation system to Amelia Island, and the town was inhabited by a large number of slaves harvesting, among other commodities, indigo.

Indigo was a main export crop for British Florida, but it was a nasty business for the slaves who worked it. Boiling indigo smelled putrid, gave off toxic fumes, and there was an account written by a Revolutionary War soldier, claiming that indigo, "on average killed every Negro employed in its culture in the short pace of five years." Nevertheless, it was a cash crop, along with sugar, sea cotton, and rice.

Then the Embargo Act of 1807 terminated trade between America and Britain. Tired of British and French piracy of US cargo ships, President Jefferson said, "We're putting our ships in port. We're not going to trade with anyone." That cut America off from coffee, tea, sugar, rum and wine.

The Embargo Act didn't have the effect Jefferson intended. Instead, Amelia Island became the biggest coastal smuggling operation in America, run almost exclusively by pirates. Pirates enabled the smuggling, yet the pirates didn't keep records, and the US government wasn't paying attention. Piracy was a lucrative business that went on for quite a while. There were written reports that up to 200 sailing ships could be seen at one time anchored in the island's deep harbors, even at low tide. There were smugglers from as far away as Russia.

Pirates ran the illegal trade and they ran the town, which at that point consisted of a long vacant lot and six or seven bordellos. In addition to these illegal activities, pirates continued to import slaves from the Caribbean and sell them fresh off the docks in Fernandina Beach. In 1783, the second Treaty of Paris handed the island back to Spain. But Spanish power was waning by 1811.

At that point in history, President James Madison was ready to initiate his own action against the pirates dominating one of the deepest harbors in the southeast coast. He appropriated $100,000 and contacted General George Matthews, a former governor of Georgia, advising him to recruit 200 men. "Call them the Patriots," the president said.

Seventy "Patriots" from Georgia and Florida tried to take over the island for the United States covertly backed by the US president. The general's men came to Fernandina in two American gunboats and docked in the harbor. A local man rowed out to meet them. "What do you want?" he asked.

The general replied, "We want to take over your town."

The next day the Patriot flag was raised in Spanish territory. Spanish King Charles II challenged President Madison to a duel and threatened war. Madison denied any knowledge of the affair and blamed the whole thing on Matthews, who died six months later en route to Washington; it was rumored that he, too, was on his way to challenge Madison to a duel. The whole enterprise was to no avail. Spain raised its flag again.

Five years later, Gregor MacGregor, a Scottish-born veteran of several Latin-American revolutions, convinced Americans in Savannah, Georgia, that he could deliver Fernandina harbor to them in exchange for cash. The men in Savannah hedged their bets—they funded MacGregor, but they also sent a spy to warn the town of Fernandina.

In June of 1817, MacGregor docked at Egans Creek with 150 men, including some veterans of the 1812 war. Decked out in their uniforms, which included plumed hats, the veterans looked like officers and they easily gained possession of the harbor and the town. Their flag was white with a green cross and it flew over the island until September. By then, "The Republic of Floridas" was dead broke and insidious rebellion forced MacGregor to resort to piracy to keep his small government afloat. President James Monroe was involved in sensitive negotiations with Spain, and he was no help to the fledgling administration. MacGregor abandoned the town, went to sea, and became a full-time pirate.

Exit one pirate, enter another. Luis Aury, a notorious mercenary, strode ashore and claimed the island for the Mexican Revolution. The Mexican flag duly flew over the land as Aury stepped up illegal slave trade, bringing over 1,000 slaves a month to the Fernandina harbor. Spain could not protect northeast Florida from a man like Aury, but US troops did. They kicked Aury out within a year and held the island "in trust" for Spain. Aury left behind a son, Luc, who was as bad as he was. See the ghost story of Bosque Bello cemetery in Chapter 17.

History continued to unravel in Nassau County at a rapid pace. In 1821, the United States promised Spain five million dollars, which it never paid, in exchange for the island. Senator David Yulee moved Old Town to accommodate the first cross-country railroad in Fernandina in the 1850s, yet he gets little credit for the train because of his Confederate sympathies, which landed him in jail during the Civil War.

In 1861, the Confederate Army took over Fort Clinch (Chapter 19) for a year, and then abandoned it. The fort was retained for the Union for the duration of the Civil War.

After the turn of the century, tourism went southward in northeast Florida. The Great Depression did little to boost its allure to consumptive tourists and flashy New Dealers with pockets of cash, although the film industry, bootleggers, and Cuban insurgents briefly took notice.

Today, Jacksonville retains the grandeur of its past with the modern accoutrements of a major Florida University (University of North Florida), beautiful beaches, a booming shrimping industry, and tourist trade. Baker County holds an annual Civil War reenactment on a real battle site, but other than that, is basically known for its proximity to federal prisons incarcerating death row prisoners. Clay and Flagler counties, basically bedroom communities today, never regained their dominance in the tourist trade, although they are a well-kept secret among Florida insiders and well-known camp sites for scouting organizations.

Nassau County sponsors a broad span of tourist attractions from their annual Eight Flags Shrimp Festival to their "Talk Like a Pirate Day" sponsored by the Fernandina Beach Pirates Club. A civic organization, and sponsor of several charitable projects, its members can usually be found hanging out at the Palace saloon in full costume, spouting pirate dialect.

And there you have it: Indians, pirates, revolutionaries, US diplomats and presidents, slaves, plantation owners, prostitutes, and mercenaries. Buried treasure still lies hidden in the fertile soil, unmarked by maps long crumbled with age. Enemies are interred side by side in local graveyards, and watery galleons surface at night to search the Gulf Stream. There are many secrets in northeast Florida, secrets told in the coded language of ghost lore, guarded by the presence of Women in White.

Now it's time to begin.

FLAGLER COUNTY

Chapter 1

PRINCESS PLACE PRESERVE

This just used to be a place I would go. To play.

—**Gail Wadsworth**

The Haunting

Gail Wadsworth is the clerk of the county court in Flagler County, and the niece of Lewis Wadsworth, who owned the grounds of Princess Place in the 1950s and '60s. She played there often as a child and actually met the namesake of the preserve: Princess Angela Scherbatoff. Wadsworth is convinced the house and the grounds are haunted. She gave three examples:

- First, the triangular closet in the princess's former bedroom has a peculiar connection with water. According to Wadsworth, an Indian woman touring the facility stepped into the closet and came out with dripping-wet hands. "There's death in there," the woman said darkly.
- Second, Wadsworth relates that another closet, with ladder access to the loft, is haunted. "We used to get to the third step," she says, "and something would bump us. Always on the left side. It happened to me and to my sister."
- Third, Royce Mitchell, a park ranger who gives tours at the Princess Place Preserve, confirmed Wadsworth's story of the woman in the closet with the dripping-wet hands. Then he added a twist. Mitchell says:

I was giving a tour the year before last and there was this old couple on the tour. The old guy was standing by the door. A lady in rain gear, all wet, came in, standing in between the husband and his wife. She walked behind everyone when we left, but…the old guy never saw her leave. She just disappeared.

Who was the mysterious ghost? Was it the prince? The princess? An Indian? A soldier? How did it die, who killed it, and how long will it remain? These questions remain a mystery at Princess Place Preserve.

The trees of Princess Place Preserve are grotesquely twisted from hurricane winds.

The History

Like all fairy-tale princesses, the Princess Place Preserve underwent many transformations before becoming a premier Flagler County state park situated on Pellicer Creek and the Matanzas River (called "The Flats" by natives). Originally, the 1,100-acre Spanish land grant was acquired in 1791 by Francisco Pellicer, a Minorcan carpenter who lived in St. Augustine. At that time, the land was part of St. Johns County. Orange groves were planted there in the early 1800s, and the land was worked for the timber and turpentine.

In 1886, Henry Cutting purchased the land and named it Cherokee Grove. He built an Adirondack-style hunting lodge—without electricity or running water—out of topical materials such as pink coquina, tabby, pine, cedar, and palm trunks. He furnished it with rattan and wicker. The lodge is a one-of-a kind design.

Cutting also built a livery stable, two bathhouses, tennis courts and a fresh water swimming pool. His largess must have impressed his attractive black-haired and blue-eyed bride, Angela Mills, a former maid who lived in a New York hotel. Mills clearly had higher aspirations, and a taste for dashing men, and she realized both with Cutting, enjoying family life and entertaining at the hunting lodge, their home away from home.

Wadsworth says that Henry Cutting died in 1892 in a boat headed to St. Augustine, seeking treatment for a snakebite. His widow, left with two small children but plenty of money, married a philandering stockbroker, J. L. Worden, in 1901. She stuck it out almost twenty years before she divorced him, no doubt enriched by the settlement. Her accumulated largess did not, however, extend to family life. Sadly, she lost both of her sons, one to disease, and the other, a few years after her divorce, in an automobile accident.

Things were looking up for Angela Mills Cutting Worden in 1923, when she met the alleged exiled Russian prince, Boris Scherbatoff, who may or may not have been thrown out of his homeland after the Bolshevik revolution for reasons unknown. Apparently, he feared for his life, because he changed his name to Scherbatow, when he and his presumptuous princess settled in the isolated hunting lodge she inherited from her first husband. It was around this time that his bride, at the age of fifty-nine, assumed the title of "Princess" and the 1,500 acres of pristine woodlands became known as "Princess Place." By now, the preserve was situated in newly named Flagler County, established from portions of St. Johns and Volusia Counties.

The prince died in 1949, and the Princess, a widow once again, stayed on at the hunting lodge, but traveled extensively, purchasing quantities of goods and furnishings. Wadsworth says:

> *There were tapestries from Iran. As a child, I could go up there [in the loft] and hide forever. This place was always glutted with furniture. The dining room was filled with barrels-unopened. She [the princess] loved to shop.*

Livery stable at Princess Place Preserve.

Wadsworth met the princess three times and described her as a woman who always "wore black, a hat, and lots of jewelry." A childless woman, she also allowed the youngsters free access to her library. Wadsworth says, "The rule was if you bring the book back, you can borrow another. If you could tell her [the princess] about the book, you can keep it. She always paid more attention to the children than to their parents."

Two years before her death, in 1954, at the age of ninety, the princess sold Princess Place to Wadsworth's aunt and uncle, who promptly converted the gun and ammo room into a bathroom with indoor plumbing and wired the house for electricity. When Wadsworth's uncle died, the estate sold to another couple, the Kittredges and, in the 1990s, it passed on to the Flagler County Board of County Commissioners. Governor Lawton Chiles dedicated it as a preserve in 1994, and Flagler County eventually bought its surrounding lands. Donna Wadsworth Katz, an historian and Wadsworth's cousin-in-law, still lives on the grounds.

The road to Princess Place reserve is lined with groves of pine trees planted in rows where bald eagles sometimes roust. Wild deer frolic in the woods. There is an equestrian trailhead, a golf course, a picnic area, and campgrounds replete with Southern Magnolia trees and Muscadine grape vines. Wadsworth says that the landscaping of the preserve is the same as it was a half century ago when she and her playmates used to "play Tarzan on the vines." Yet there are signs of the passage of time. Trees close to Pellicer Creek are stunted and mutated into grotesque shapes by the wind. The bathhouses lean precariously these days, but the spring-fed pool is maintained and the livery stable, which houses an old buggy and a hog-scalding pot, is often the site of local weddings.

The main attraction is the hunting lodge, which bears a faint odor of mold eclipsed by the hand-carved molding, hard pine floors, and tiled fireplaces. The doors are put together in panels in the old tongue-and-groove style without nails. A huge pool table dominates the dining area, and a spacious loft, formerly filled with barrels of goods from the princess's shopping sprees, circles the entire room. The kitchen and the butler's pantry, originally the only rooms with running water, still house the original stove. According to Wadsworth, the princess never let the stove go out. "It was her only source of hot water."

The lodge has eight bedrooms: four main bedrooms with smaller adjoining servant's rooms. The master bedroom, which Wadsworth says was painted white when the princess reigned, overlooks a wraparound porch with rocking chairs and a dock leading out to the creek. Don Deal, a longtime resident, reminisces that the kids used to catch fish in the little estuaries.

At the Princess Place Preserve, a museum exhibit is in the works thanks to a grant from the Tourist Development Council. The waters of Pellicer Creek are part of the State Canoe trail, while across the way looms Flagler County's Marineland. Each maintains a queer juxtaposition of the environmental attractions of Flagler County. Timacuan Indians used to paddle Pellicer's shores, seeking the distinct pink coquina indigenous to the landscape. Today, Boy Scouts and tourists do the same, taking in the sight of the preserve from every angle. It is still the largest intact land grant from the first Spanish Period, but like all things, possessions change hands, people rise and fall and die off. It is the fluidity of water and death that the preserve ghost stories allude to, and it is the surrounding water and the royal ghost of its past that enhance the essence of Princess Place Preserve.

Visitor Information

Princess Place Preserve
2500 Princess Place Road
Palm Coast, FL 32137
www.flaglercounty.org/facilities.aspx?page=detail&RID=18

CLAY COUNTY

Chapter 2

The Old Clay County Jail

My mama always told me never put off till tomorrow people you can kill today.
—**Dennis Quaid** as Doc Holliday in *Wyatt Earp*

The Haunting

As told by Visitra R. Garig, volunteer researcher and docent for the Clay County Archives:

> *So me and Lisa, one of the other volunteers, were standing in the booking room one morning—we had the jail registers out. We were going through them, looking for court cases on the executions we've had here. I'm standing here...and we were talking about one particular defendant, a guy named Ed Douglas. In 1904, he raped his seven-year-old stepdaughter and gave her syphilis. Ed Douglas was held here in this jail.*
>
> *We were talking about him and what a dirt bag he was, and both of us heard a male voice, right over there [by the door]. He was just mumbling; he was unintelligible. I said to Lisa, "Did you hear that?" And she said, "Yeah, I heard that." I said, "Quick, get outside and see if anyone's going by on the sidewalk."*
>
> *We ran outside, and there was no one there.*

Despite the irreverent streak of blue in her hair, Garig is bursting with information and has obviously delved deep into many of the 40,000 archives housed in the old Clay County Jail. She is also a former member of a paranormal team, which is how she discovered the jail in the first place. These days, trios looking for orbs and apparitions are charged by the county to book time to set up their equipment in the old jail. According to Garig, it's almost always worth it.

Alone in the building, she has heard coughing, echoes, footsteps, and jail cell doors creaking open. She has been locked out of the main building twice when she left for a bathroom break. She says that other people have heard music, singing, and smelled perfume. These events occur at all hours of the day and night.

Garig climbs up the original steel stairs of the jail past a rusty old radiator to the upper left corridor of the 6,000 square foot cellblock. Her voice echoes. "People experience physical contact," Garig says. "Their hair is pulled, they get scratches. The spirits are very interactive."

She walks past a row of cells to a window with names carved in the wooden sill. The sunlight is weak and cheerless on the cellblock, but the crudely carved name Elizabeth displays prominently. Garig says, "That must have been poor Lizzie Sheffield who died here. A bit *teched* in the head as they said."

The upper right corridor of the cellblock was the maximum-security ballast of the old jail where the most dangerous and violent prisoners were housed. Recently, a writer, staring down the row of cells, heard her Smartpen inexplicably come on. A Smartpen is a writing tool that allows a writer to take notes and to record conversations at the same time. Users have to mash an "on" button and wait a minute for it to start up. In the Old Clay County Jail, the Smartpen was playing back the recorded conversation that Garig was conducting in the old jail. Recordings never play back unless the user touches the pen to a particular point of the LiveScribe note paper that comes with the Smartpen.

Perhaps the tinny device invokes the voice of poor dead Elizabeth and all the other lost and abandoned souls locked up with men who were drunks, murderers, child rapists—desperate, depraved men, more animals than human beings. In the grim and isolated jailhouse, there were also the sounds of footsteps on the gallows, and a trap door opening. These creepy elements have brewed in the old jail since 1894.

Concocting what?

Garig, and another local historian, Claude Bass, compile ghost cams of nights in the cellblock. In one, something keeps blocking the camera mouth although Garig asserts that there was no one there. Apparently, this is bona fide paranormal stuff; a local television station filmed its pilot episode here. *Local Haunts*, at the jail.

Still, the ghosts of the Old Clay County Jail pale in comparison to its history.

The History

Heading into Green Cove Springs, the county seat of Clay County, the St. Johns River commands the vista, curving, widening, reflecting the greenery of the trees closest to shore. The downtown area includes Spring Park, its gazebo, and a warm artesian sulfur-scented mineral spring, which flows into a public swimming pool and then winds its way into the St. Johns River.

1894 OLD COUNTY JAIL
CLAY COUNTY
ARCHIVES
&
HISTORICAL RESOURCE
CENTER
OPERATED BY
JAMES B. JETT
CLERK OF THE CIRCUIT COURT

The Old Clay County Jail and the parking lot where the gallows used to stand.

Green Cove Springs was a tourist spot, at least until the Great Depression, with steamboat landings and fancy hotels. It held a naval air station during World War II, and after the war, it contained a fleet of 600 navy boats along thirteen piers down the length of the St. Johns River. Nowadays, it's a small city with under 6,000 working-class residents.

These images belied the early twentieth century underside of Green Cove Springs, which was all about poverty, moonshine, and turpentine. The haunted site tourists love to discover the Old Clay County Jail is legend to a violent and depraved history, which sprang from extreme poverty.

Below the surface of the tourist industry, the underclass of Green Cove Springs had a thriving moonshine racket. On Friday nights, milk trucks and fuel tankers came to Clay County to pick up the illegal hooch and deliver it to Miami.

"It was like the wild west here at the turn of the century," says Vishitra R. Garig. She talks casually of murder and moonshiners, and desperate crimes.

> *We've had three sheriffs killed in the line of duty. In 1913, Deputy Theodore Cherry was shot full of holes by moonshiners. They brought him back here and he bled to death in the booking room. When the floor was torn up for renovations in the '70s, we found blood stains soaked into the wood.*

But it is the sight of the jail that is jolting: a whitewashed brick building with a paper mache mannequin in black stripes dangling from a cell window. One of the oldest continually operating jails in Florida, it was built in 1894 by the Pauly Jail Company, the same outfit that constructed the Old St. Augustine jail and Alcatraz.

The Old Clay County Jail housed prisoners until 1972. The parking lot in the rear of the jail is the site of its former gallows, a miniature of which is available for viewing in the old booking room. At different times, five men mounted the gallows, dropped, swung, and cast an oscillating shadow upon the now-innocuous clearing.

The main building, the oldest part, is high ceilinged and full of antique bottles, along with an old radio and camera, and a Plantation desk from Georgia. The adjacent booking room holds the old jail records, and the "Lunacy Book" of court proceedings for committing the insane who had no relatives to claim them. They were taken to the Chattahoochee mental ward; one such inmate, Elizabeth Shriver, died in the jail in 1939 while awaiting transport.

The booking room displays standing and glass encased artifacts: blackjacks, billy clubs, moonshine stills, handcuffs, scraps of paper used for playing cards, jail keys, files, an old courthouse chair, and weapons taken off prisoners.

Close-up of convict mannequin.

The maximum security wing in the upper right corridor.

"One prisoner slit his own throat with a piece of tin," Garig explains.

The cellblock was built in 1903 to afford the deputies, who lived in the main building, some privacy from the inmates. The jail cells are about ten feet by ten feet with their original plumbing and heating. Lead paint peels on the eighteen-inch thick walls. The floors are the original concrete from the early twentieth century. Rusty, barred doors guard eerie paper mache prisoners who sit or stand.

"They're from the old St. Augustine jail," Garig says. "Hollow, but filled with cockroaches, probably."

A rear, corner cell once housed Abram Middleton, a murderer who was hanged in the parking lot in 1912. Tourists can see the barred window where the guards placed a chair on the other side for his wife during visits. Middleton committed an interesting crime when viewed through the lens of Florida's current gun laws. He was a moonshiner who refused to sell his whiskey to some men who wanted to buy it. The men harassed Middleton, returning to his store a few times, tempers escalating. Finally, Middleton, feeling threatened or offended, aimed, shot, and killed one of them. Middleton was convicted of premeditated murder and executed in short order.

Visitor Information

The Old Clay County Jail
21 Gratio Place & S. R. 16
Green Cove Springs, FL 32043
http://archives.clayclerk.com/ghosts.html

DUVAL COUNTY

Chapter 3

The Florida Theatre

I like entertaining people. I really miss it.
—**Elvis Presley**

The Haunting

In the early 1900s, Jacksonville, once known as "The World's Winter Film Capital," opened a dozen movie "palaces" downtown, which took up whole blocks of the city. Of these, only the magnificent eighty-five-year-old Florida Theatre, with its elaborate Moorish architecture and décor, survives. According to Tiffani Irish, a Florida Theatre employee and our tour guide, the theater is also haunted.

Irish takes individual and group tours through the theatre, past a row of plum-colored seats in the curved sloping balcony, row B, where employees and theatergoers often see a figure sitting there...who vanishes. She shows the Barnett room, which used to be a nursery for the performers' children; it is also the site where she had a personal experience with the supernatural entities of the theatre.

The Barnett Room is a lovely space where the performers eat their meals from a green marble counter, with a view of the city framed by arched windows. On the wall of the room hangs an old black-and-white picture of a nurse presiding over several cribs. On the other side of that wall is a kitchen. There is only one door into the kitchen.

One day, Irish and a coworker walked into the Barnett Room, and all the lights in the kitchen inexplicably went out. Keeping the door open, Irish and her companion cautiously walked toward the kitchen through the hallway. As they did, the hallway light went out. She and her friend bolted.

One would think that power outages were common in an old building. Yet, Irish said none of the switches flipped nor were there any other outages or electrical problems.

Although a myriad of explanations would suffice for Irish's "paranormal" experience, the best one has to do with a certain Memphis megastar who performed at the Florida Theatre in 1956. He was well known not only for his

A view from the balcony and the orchestra pit of the Florida Theatre.

music and for his suggestive hip gyrations, but also for kitchen forages, featuring his beloved peanut butter and banana sandwiches. But that was a long time ago, and, at best, an unlikely scenario for the absence of light in the Barnett Room's kitchen. Or perhaps not. Sightings of this long-dead performer continue to accumulate.

Perhaps Elvis has never left the building.

The History

In the early twentieth century, the Radio City Music Hall in New York City, a great theater, featured news shorts and a stage show, accompanied by a band number from the orchestra pit, and a feature film. The Florida Theatre followed the same format. Although "talkie" films began to gain popularity the same year the theater opened, some of the Florida Theatre's earliest film offerings included silent films, which starred Oliver Hardy, Fatty Arbuckle, Tom Mix, and Lionel and Ethel Barrymore. Dignitaries, celebrities and local politicians used the theater

The Florida Theatre box office and evidence of the Bricks and Bars Star campaign for supporters.

as a social and a political forum. In 1928, a popular long-term Jacksonville politician, Mayor John Alsop, celebrated his birthday at the Florida Theatre with "a double decker cake."

Costly to maintain, the upkeep on the theater was unending. According to Duval County Property Records, the building, which has an unfinished basement, is over seven stories tall and just under 75,000 square feet. In the late 1960s, the Florida Theater was closed as the advent of the lavish movie theaters ended, and the immense building languished in disrepair.

By 1983, however, money from local philanthropists, grants, and a promotional campaign, enabled the Jacksonville Cultural Council to renovate and restore the aging theater.

Today, the theater, listed on the National Register of Historic Places, no longer shows movies, but it still has an impressive roster of live performers. Typically, the theatre hosts four or five shows a month. Some of them, past and present, were historic.

Radio City may have had the dancing Rockettes, but the Florida Theatre also, famously, provided the forum for Elvis Presley's first live performance. Country music singer Faith Hill unveiled her solo debut at the Florida Theatre in 1996, as did the *American Idol* winner Taylor Hicks in 2007.

The experience of stepping inside the incredibly elaborate building, and wandering among the plush, ornate, intricate fountains, arches, and balconies is like stepping back to a celebrated evening that occurred almost a century ago. The original heating elements are still under the seats whose rows preserve ornate labeling and elaborate wrought iron railings with a coat of arms. A panel of buttons on the wall upstairs retains the remnants of a once-elaborate seating system.

The theater itself is built to hold 1,800 theatergoers, and the building overwhelms the senses with size, color, design, and texture. From the ceiling, carved with wooden frescoes, hang huge lowering lamps. Still, there are undeniable signs of wear.

The lobby is decorated with hanging starlights, but the original lead glass in the ticket booth is broken. In the theater, the original plum-colored seats are somewhat worn, threadbare, and taped to contain tears. Upstairs, in the balcony, the floor slants where the building is still settling, and paint is worn away on the banisters. Walking is more like staggering. "I never wear heels up here," Irish confides.

Friends of the Florida Theatre, a volunteer organization, help to keep costs down by recruiting ushers as volunteers. They also sponsor events, such as their annual "Art After Dark" where the works of old, new, and student artists are displayed in the lobby, thus showcasing and reintroducing the theater to a new generation of patrons.

So many nights of entertainment have accumulated at the Florida Theatre. Almost every significant performer, lecturer, musician, and comedian of the past twenty years has performed there. Black-and-white pictures display the long lines of pubescent fans waiting in line to see Elvis Presley. According to a Florida Theatre brochure, "a city judge was called to sit front and center to ensure that no lewd act…or otherwise bawdy behavior might misguide or offend the good senses of those in the audience."

Each event represents an era of entertainment that comes, goes, and never comes again. Impressive and grand, the Florida Theater still stands as the body of the live performance; its essence, of course, is the performer, the heart of the Florida Theatre. And the beat goes on…

Visitor Information

The Florida Theatre
128 East Forsyth Street
Jacksonville, FL 32202
www.floridatheatre.com

Chapter 4

JACKSONVILLE HISTORY MUSEUM AND ARCHIVES

(Old St. Luke's Hospital)

The calmer you are, the better you can help this Committee to execute its plans for your relief.

—Colonel J. J. Daniel
Chairman, Auxiliary Sanitation Committee
August,1888

The Haunting

The present Jacksonville Historical Museum's Archives Building is really the old St. Luke's Hospital, built in 1878 to house consumptive tourists, then to contain victims of an 1888 yellow fever epidemic, and a decade later, to tend to a typhoid outbreak. Since the mortality rates from the epidemics were so high, small wonder then, that there is a brick building in the parking lot of the old hospital, which was once called the Florida Casket Factory.

The Casket Factory had a chute from the factory to the hospital wings in case a casket was needed. Clearly, sensitivity to the fears and feelings of the dying was not a distinguishing characteristic of hospitals in those days. For example, in St. Augustine's Old Spanish Military Hospital, workers began nailing the coffin together in the Mourning Room soon after expiring soldiers were wheeled in there to die. In the case of St. Luke's Hospital, it is logical to assume that sometimes the casket arrived in the patient's room before she was quite dead from whatever deadly disease, consumption, yellow fever, or typhoid, ailed her.

In spite of the scores of patients who have died in the old building, Jacksonville Historical Society archivist, Lauren Mosley, said she's noticed nothing unusual during her brief sojourn there, and she could only come up with one ghost story. The story concerned a former hospital patient, dead of yellow fever, dressed in black, who roamed the old hospital wringing her hands,

All that remains of the Old St. Luke's Hospital in the city of Jacksonville.

crying and screaming because one of the Casket Company's coffins chuted into her room. Since then, she's been haunting the old hospital.

Hauling a casket into patient's sickroom was insensitive, but the ghost of Old St. Luke's Hospital sounds a little histrionic, not to mention impractical. Faulkner's fictional Addie Bundren put up with sounds of mournful carpentry as she lay dying.

Even though it failed to contain her spirit, the wailing ghost of St. Luke's Hospital clearly needed the coffin at some point.

The History

The present structure on Palmetto is the third of three buildings named after St. Luke, patron saint of physicians and surgeons. The first St. Luke's Hospital was a two-room building erected in the 1870s to accommodate tourists with tuberculosis who came to Jacksonville to enjoy the nice weather and stayed to sicken and to die. It was too small. A larger St. Luke's was built, but it burned down. The structure presently on Palmetto Avenue went up in 1878. By 1884, St. Luke's Hospital opened a nursing school where nurses boarded in the attic, attended classes, and tended the sick.

Within a few years, they had plenty of work on their hands. St. Luke's Hospital had three wards, each of which held up to ten patients and twelve rooms that easily held more. In 1888, St. Luke's was one of the primary hospitals used for the yellow fever epidemic (the other was Sand-Hill). Events of that horrific time between July and November 1888 were thoroughly documented in the records of "The Auxiliary Sanitation Committee" of Jacksonville, an interim government, who took over the management of the 14,000 citizens who were left after most of the white population, including some elected city officials, fled the scourge of the fever. The committee kept order, raised funds, fed destitute citizens, organized health care, and provided work. Their work was daunting and exhausting even when its members were in the best of health, which was rarely the case. Many of their members fell ill or died from yellow fever. At times, they had trouble assembling a quorum.

The Jacksonville yellow fever epidemic began when a businessman, visiting from Tampa and ensconced in a local hotel, fell ill from yellow fever (he consequently recovered). The pervasive disease permeated Jacksonville. Soon, the streets outside St. Luke's Hospital represented a scene from Dante's *Inferno*. Panic reigned. Cannons went off at regular intervals, sometimes 200 times in one day, because the "concussion theory" held that the gunpowder "killed the microbes." Malodorous pine and tar fires burned for the same purpose, and mail from Jacksonville was "fumigated" before it was delivered elsewhere. All Jacksonville newspapers were banned by neighboring counties, so concerned relatives had to rely on the telegraph to get news. Soldiers guarded the homes of victims whose doors were adorned with a yellow flag. All of Jacksonville's precautions were in vain; no one knew that mosquitoes transmitted the yellow fever until Walter Reed's research around the turn of the century.

There were stories of hungry orphans roaming the street, as their parents lay dead in their beds. A clerk committed suicide by swallowing laudanum. A wedding concluded with a bride coming down with yellow fever and the groom sending for a doctor "in the same carriage that took the clergyman home." Because of its accessibility, the worst cases went to St. Luke's. Patients were often deathly ill by the time they got there, giving St. Luke's a higher death record than other hospitals.

State Treasurer of Florida Henry L'Engle, relative to famous author Madeline L'Engle, is documented as being on the auxiliary sanitation committee and donating $100 of his own money toward the relief of yellow fever victims. He was one of a dozen yellow fever casualties on September 14, a day labeled "Black Friday" in the auxiliary records.

Clara Barton, nurse heroine and president of the American Red Cross, telegraphed the auxiliary committee in September, inquiring, "Do you want the assistance of the Red Cross with experienced yellow fever nurses?" Complaining of "intoxicated" and "inefficient" local nurses, the committee readily agreed. Nurse Barton dispatched her nurses immediately, but trains would not enter the city. So the nurses jumped from a moving train and made their way on foot to the beleaguered city and to St. Luke's Hospital.

Once there, they were treated less than cordially, and two were asked to leave because they wouldn't follow the instructions of the auxiliary committee. Of course, by that time it was almost impossible to leave or to enter Jacksonville because of the statewide quarantine and cordons blocking the borders.

A soothing presence throughout the epidemic and panic was evidenced by the "Colored Auxiliary Committee" (CAB), a group of citizens who served soup to the destitute, cleaned up, and performed the manual labor neglected by the city as most workers had fled, died, or lay ill. Unfortunately, their ranks were the first cut from rations when the Auxiliary Sanitation Committee started economizing in mid-October.

However, by October the number of yellow fever cases was declining, which made sense because the weather was cooling off and the mosquitoes, breeding in cisterns and other vehicles of standing water, were less abundant. Still the number of people who succumbed to yellow fever was substantial and the auxiliary report ledger of the dead included the name of the president of the Auxiliary Sanitation Committee, Colonel J. J. Daniels.

By late November, when the temperature dropped to 32° and killed all of the mosquitoes, nearly 5,000 Jacksonville citizens had contracted the disease, and over 400 died. Many people chose to die at home, and the committee sent nurses and doctors to tend them. The Jacksonville Auxiliary

Sanitation Committee report also lists people who succumbed to yellow fever within the walls of St. Luke's, about 40 people in all.

What is left today, functioning as the Jacksonville Historical Society's Archives, is the original core of the hospital. It is a pleasant, light-filled building, decidedly unspooky, whose walls are muted shades of mauve and beige.

Old St. Luke's Hospital forayed into Jacksonville politics at one point. The building was Congresswoman Karen Brown's headquarters, and then it became the offices of Senator Charlie Bennett. In fact, the small library and reading room bears a plaque over the fireplace inscribed as the "Bennett Reading Room."

The final structure, built in 1878, still stands today minus the wings. The city has grown up around the two-story brick building with its veranda and cupola, which looks very much as it did in the nineteenth century, although the demolishment of the wings has kept the building off the State and National Historic Registry. Nevertheless, the building preserves, somewhat in disarray because of the recent move, documents, photographs, maps, diaries, etc., all of which tell the absorbing stories of a city of unprecedented growth, beleaguered by disease, and recovered through hard work and courage.

The fact that many of these stories are collected and condensed into the actual building, which was at the center of a lot of its history, endows relevance and a reality to past events that is downright eerie. One can imagine the rattle of the death carts collecting yellow fever victims and the boom of cannons as citizens walk past the old Casket Factory, adjacent to the museum. Both are dwarfed by the modernism of a twenty-first century city.

The wailing "lady in black" story of Old St. Luke's Hospital is an echo of Jacksonville's authentic voice. However, at this late date, there are no signs that she is ever going to take Colonel Daniel's advice and calm down.

Visitor Information

Jacksonville Historical Society/ Old St. Luke's' Hospital
314 Palmetto Avenue
Jacksonville, FL 32202
www.jaxhistory.com/archives.htm

Chapter 5

The Kingsley Plantation

The cotton is quite forward and now begins to blossom.

—Kingsley Beatty Gibbs
His Journal of 1840-1843

The Haunting

There are many ghost stories connected with the Kingsley Plantation on Fort George Island in Duval County. The most well known is the story, often repeated, of the former plantation slave with an evil red gaze, who tortured, raped, mutilated and killed several slave girls until he was caught and hung, impromptu, from a nearby oak tree. Presumably, Old Red Eyes still chases women up the three-mile stretch of tree-lined palms, but he never does anything except scare them.

According to a *Folio Weekly* back-page editorial, published in January 2012, a University of Florida archeologist discovered six slave graves on the Kingsley Plantation. Whether one of the graves contained a virulent spirit is unknown. Lynn Wilbanks, a retired history teacher and live-in volunteer at the National Park, says:

> *Our official position is that it's not real. I live upstairs, [from the old clubhouse], and it's pretty isolated. I've never seen anything. We have a joke here...if you see red lights in the middle of the night, don't worry. They're just ghost hunters.*

Another benign ghost spotting is the standard "Woman in White" phenomenon. Lynn reported that a tourist told her about such a specter, presumably the protoplasm of Ana Kingsley, at the edge of the coastline. Lynn says:

> *What the ghost hunters really ought to look at is this clubhouse [The Fort George Island Visitor Center]. It was built in 1927 during prohibition, so you can imagine what went on. Winston Churchill stayed here.*

Actually, Lynn is on to something, although it is eons before the partying of the portly prime minister. According to the Timucuan Ecological and Historical

The Kingsley Plantation on St. George's Island.

Preserve, the old clubhouse, part of the Saturiwa Trail, which loops around the Kingsley Plantation was built over "prehistoric shell refuse. Archeologists estimate a "probable occupation over 4,000 years ago." These are the ancestors of ancestors to the Timucuan Indians. What spiritual beliefs permeate these ancient grounds?

Environmental writer Bill Belleville may have discovered a clue when he wrote about the seventeenth century linguist and Spanish priest Francisco Pareja who lived among the Timucuans on Fort George Island. Pareja taught the Indians to read and write and translated their legends. Pareja learned that the tribes believed each person has three souls:

> *One is the pupil of the eye, the second is the shadow the body casts, and the third is the image reflected in clear water. Upon death, two of the souls leave the body while the one in the eye remains. It is this enduring soul that is visited at the burial mound by those still living, a spirit to whom questions are addressed—and from whom counsel is received.*

Another prospective cause of supernatural activity was discovered during an archeology dig by a University of Florida professor and some of his students in 2007. They were trying to locate two of the "lost" slave cabins on the forefront of the Kingsley plantation and searching for artifacts that would demonstrate whether the slaves continued to practice their African customs on Florida soil. They unearthed an intact skeleton of a chicken, located where they believed the threshold of the cabin stood. Was this proof of an animal sacrifice celebrating an African ceremony? Or more to the point: Did the Africans conjure spirits during their enslavement on the Kingsley Plantation?

Regardless, the Kingsley Plantation has it all: Old Red Eyes, Ana Kingsley, the enduring souls of the Timucans, and African magic. But for some tourists, such a plethora of ancient commingling history is not enough. As one enigmatic guest [Voldemort, Hogwarts, UK] wrote in the Registry of National Park Visitors, "Harry Potter wasn't here."

The History

Led Zeppelins' "Stairway to Heaven" is an appropriate prologue on the way to Fort George Island Cultural State Park, where the Kingsley Plantation is located. Although a nuclear power plant squats east of the plantation, it is easy to forget all that during the long drive down the road to the plantation, which is lined by palm trees planted by the slaves of Ana Kingsley over 200 years ago.

The island is 1,000 acres of wetlands, with impossibly twisted cedar trees, that also houses the plantation house where Zephaniah lived, the kitchen house where Ana lived, a dock, a dirt floored church, the remains of twenty-five slave quarters, the old clubhouse, a well with a round wooden cover nailed shut, monarch butterflies, a birding trail, and gopher tortoise burrows. There are historic markers for self-guided tours, and a mini museum in Ana's house.

Kingsley slave quarters with tabby walls designed in a distinctive horseshoe pattern.

Before English slave trader Zephaniah Kingsley bought the plantation in 1814, previous owners produced indigo and Sea Island cotton, primarily through slave labor. Zephaniah discontinued the toxic and often fatal practice of indigo processing, (although a display of the equipment remains), but he continued to use slave labor for sugar cane and cotton. However, it was the coastline, convenient for unloading illegal slaves, which drew Zephaniah to Fort George Island.

The irony of Zephaniah's profession, which tantalizes historians to this day, is that he met Ana Madgigine, a Senegal princess, in Cuba where she was on the auction block as a captured slave. He bought her and married her. There is a prurient repulse factor to this historic attraction: Zephaniah was forty-one years old, and Ana was an adolescent of thirteen.

She was equal to the task of managing her husband's plantation during the long absences required of a slave trader. She had her own slaves, and lived separately from her husband, in her own dwelling, as the Senegalese women of status did in her homeland. It may also have been her idea to position the slave quarters in a horseshoe shaped arc, visible from the main houses. The slave

The shoreline where Zephaniah Kingsley brought slaves ashore; also the site of ghostly sightings of Ana Kingsley.

quarters, many of them still standing in ruins today, were constructed of "tabby," a mix of sand, water, and oyster shell and impervious to fire. Each cabin contained a fireplace, a kitchen, and a sleeping quarter impossibly condensed into 150 square feet per dwelling. The drivers and slaves of higher status had slightly larger homes.

Aside from the living conditions, Zephaniah and Ana practiced "the task system" of slavery. Kingsley slaves had to complete a documented work allotment each day. Then they were free to do as they wished. Many of the slaves ran their own carpentry, trapping, or fishing businesses, earning enough money to buy their freedom.

It was the end for their way of life in 1821, when Spain ceded Florida as a territory to the United States. The US had no objection to slavery, only to intermarriage between the races and the prospect of freed slaves owning property. Zephaniah had a black wife and pampered interracial children, and there was a real possibility that his family would be sold into slavery under the new regime.

He relocated his family to what was then the Dominican Republic (and is now Haiti), but only after he wrote his famous Kingsley Treatise, where he documented the rights of Africans, exalted their superiority to whites, but reluctantly abided by the system of slavery as a "judicious balancing of evils." His reasoning was that he had, after all, to provide for his family in Haiti.

In 1839, Zephaniah sold the plantation to his nephew Kingsley Beatty Gibbs (whose first wife is buried in the St. Augustine Tolomato Cemetery). Gibbs owned the plantation until 1853.

Zephaniah made frequent visits to Haiti, but he never settled there. He died in New York. Ana Kingsley moved to Jacksonville in 1846, and lived there throughout the Civil War. She died in 1870, and was buried in an unmarked grave.

The complex history of the Kingsleys, their attachment to their land, their romance and their fates easily rivals any box office saga on film. Families tour the Kingsley Plantation, instead of Disney World, Epcot, and Universal Studios. Although rife with mosquitoes, the trip to Fort George Island is a lovely excursion deep into Florida's history and its natural lushness. Visitors experience the timbre of old Florida, a reverberation that one can only hope will continue to blossom in their children's memories.

Visitor Information

The Kingsley Plantation
11676 Palmetto Avenue
Jacksonville, FL 32226
www.nps.gov/timu/historyculture/kp.htm

Chapter 6

YELLOW BLUFF FORT HISTORIC STATE PARK

...Let us go, through certain half-deserted streets, the muttering retreats of restless nights...

—T. S. Eliot
"The Love Song of J. Alfred Prufrock"

The Haunting

A former Confederate encampment and current state park, Yellow Bluff Fort is located in the small community of New Berlin. It lies on a mound across the street from a residential neighborhood and an historic nineteenth century cemetery (see New Berlin Cemetery).

Lauren Mosley, archivist of The Jacksonville Historical Society, heard a strange story while interviewing a resident living across the street from Yellow Bluff Fort. Mosley said the elderly resident complained about ghostly "people walking across the street." Mosley said the woman told her: "On a foggy night, you can see them right in front of the fort. We see them all the time."

The History

Throughout the Civil War, soldiers built batteries and dug trenches at Yellow Bluff, hoping to repel whichever side was advancing or retreating toward Jacksonville and the St. Johns River. There is no fort, despite its name, and there never was. But hundreds of Confederate soldiers held the one-acre encampment designed by General Robert E. Lee in 1862. They abandoned the earthworks the same year and Yellow Bluff was taken over by Union soldiers off and on for the rest of the war. The 54th Massachusetts Infantry Regiment, a famous troop of black soldiers and white abolitionists, depicted in the Hollywood film *Glory*, also camped at Yellow Bluff.

Civil War cannon at Yellow Bluff Fort.

Today the site is an historic state park surrounded by ancient gnarled oak trees whose branches intertwine and litter the grounds with masses of brightly colored leaves. The air smells sweet at Yellow Bluff Fort Historic State Park. The park's steep gullies hold scrub pine, holly plants, and, probably, deep beneath layers and layers of stratified earth, the litter and remnants of Union and Confederate Civil War soldiers. The small park, located within a small rural neighborhood off Yellow Bluff Road, contains a monument, two picnic tables, and five corroded cannons mounted on concrete pedestals. The grounds are partially fenced off and there is a stern sign warning wielders of metal detectors from disturbing the grounds.

Dedication to the Confederate soldiers at Yellow Bluff Fort.

The place is so quiet and deserted, it's clear that poachers are on the honor system. There were just four parking spaces, one of them handicapped, in front of the park. Visitors climb two brick steps to reach the monument, erected by the Daughters of the Confederacy (DAR) in 1950, and dedicated to the memory of the Confederate soldiers who defended Jacksonville, 1861-1865. The monument consists of two concrete slabs rimed with mold and algae, and a metal plate, which transcribed the history of the grounds. The whole thing is inexplicably topped with a cannon ball.

There is a hilly road parallel to the park. The shadows of huge oaks make intricate patterns on the deserted road. On a bright beautiful January day in Florida, it seems very different from the history that resides there; muddled spirits who congregated when the air is thick with vapor and the ghostly wisps of cannon fire.

There is nothing spooky about Yellow Bluff Fort despite sightings of restless spirits. Leave the Electronic Voice Phenomenon (EVP) recorders at home. Instead, pack a picnic basket and bring the camera, bring the dog. The ghosts may be walking, but the birds are singing.

Visitor Information

Yellow Bluff Fort Historic State Park
Jacksonville, FL 32226
https://www.floridastateparks.org/park/Yellow-Bluff

Directions: exit Highway 9A at Hecksher Drive.
Traveling north on 9A, turn left.
Traveling south on 9A, turn right.
Take a left onto New Berlin Road.
2 miles ahead on the right.

Chapter 7

New Berlin Cemetery

Water will always run downhill.

—**Napoleon Bonaparte Broward**

The Haunting

The former governor of Florida, Napoleon Bonaparte Broward, was renowned and reviled for his plan to drain the Everglades. The plan was renowned because it led to the boom of land development that led to the city of Fort Lauderdale, and, for Floridians who've been there, the plan was reviled for the same reason. But Governor Broward understood the water. He was a boat captain in New Berlin and a coastal gunrunner for the Cuban resistance. He assumed that there was a basic physical law of water that did not change and it was this: water, left to its own devices, is always looking for the easiest route to its destination.

What humans share with water, of course, is that it comprises three quarters of our body weight. Like water, people meander ever onwards toward their destiny, intended or otherwise. So, this is not so much a ghost story as an account of a series of synchronistic events that occurred in January 2012 while Bob and I were doing fieldwork for this book.

It began on a January afternoon in a museum in Jacksonville.

I made the acquaintance of Mr. Lester A. Hardee at the Museum of Southern History. The museum itself is a well-kept facility with a good library that collects and details the Confederate end of the Civil War and then encases it in glass. There were artifacts such as the epaulettes of a famous general, a Confederate naval flag (which looked original), and a miniature reproduction of toy soldiers strategically reenacting the Florida Battle of Olustee.

Mr. Hardee informed me that his was an illustrious lineage. His great-great uncle was William J. Hardee, also known during the Civil War as "Old Reliable," a confederate general, and a former roommate of Beauregard. Lester was also

Back entrance to the New Berlin Cemetery.

the great-grandson of a former Jacksonville river rat and the nineteenth Florida governor: Napoleon Bonaparte Broward. In fact, the picture of the former governor in his prime depicted on the cover of Professor Samuel Proctor's book *Napoleon Bonaparte Broward: Florida's Fighting Democrat*, uncannily resembled Lester, right down to the moustache; that is, minus a few wrinkles, and with brown rather than white hair.

The next day, Bob and I drove to Yellow Bluff Fort Historic State Park in the small residential community of New Berlin. Across the street was Olympia Avenue and at the end of the street, hidden from the former Confederate encampment, was an old cemetery, which Bob and I found quite by accident or by instinct. We strolled down Olympia Avenue past houses with wells and barking dogs tied up outside. We found the cemetery protected with what looked like an original fence with rusty spikes and ornate iron loops. Someone was getting ready for a funeral; there was a blue tent about fifty yards away. Some maintenance guys were working, and we asked them the name of the cemetery, but they didn't know.

The gate was open; we walked right in. The first gravestone I saw was inscribed with the name Georgie Caroline Broward, wife of N. B. Broward. Next to her marker was a smaller grave with a stone lamb on top—the symbol of a dead child. This headstone was inscribed with the name Napoleon B. Broward. The infant's birth date was the day before Georgie died, and his

The grave of Georgie Caroline Broward, first wife of Florida's nineteenth governor: Napoleon Bonaparte Broward.

death occurred the day after what would have been his mother's twentieth birthday. It was clear that these two graves marked the tragic deaths of Napoleon Bonaparte Broward's first wife and his infant child—gone within nine months of marriage.

Bob and I walked back to Yellow Bluff Fort Historic State Park and sat on a bench under an oak tree. Not far away was the fishing village of New Berlin where a young Napoleon Broward piloted folks from coast to coast before he fell in love with the riverboat captain's beautiful daughter Georgiana.

Minutes later a Ford pickup pulled up and parked. Out stepped Martin Thomas, who'd just driven down from Georgia to attend the funeral across the street. He didn't know the name of the cemetery either, but he was eighty-five years old that day, January 5, and he sat with us for a while talking with a lit cigarette bobbing up and down between his lips. "I used to be a river boat captain," Martin said. "Right here on the St. Johns. Took folks to Cumberland Island."

When I got home, I got Lester A. Hardee's phone number from the curator of the Museum of Southern History. Then I called, and told him I'd stumbled across the graves of his great-grandfather's first wife and his half great-uncle. Lester was quiet a minute. "I heard that story. I heard the baby died because they couldn't get anyone to nurse it. But I never knew where they were buried."

I told him where to find the cemetery. By now, I knew it was the New Berlin Cemetery, which made sense because Georgiana was born, grew up, and married there. He said thank you, and I said you're welcome, and that was it.

I said that the tale of New Berlin cemetery wasn't a ghost story, but, in truth, I'm not so sure. Why were Bob and I drawn toward that side of the street? Why was the first headstone I walked up to that of a forgotten woman who was married to one of the most powerful men in Florida?

Napoleon Bonaparte Broward always said that water flowed downward, taking the path of least resistance. I had just shuffled through a series of unintended events, which led to, perhaps, the first person paying her respects to Georgiana and her baby in over a century. I met a former riverboat captain about to attend a funeral at the same cemetery. I knew how to get the phone number of a man who resembled and was related to Georgiana's late husband. I was able to tell this man, Lester, how to find her. I hope he does, because, if I believed in such things, I would believe that was N. B. Broward's intention.

The History

In 1860, Dr. Henry Von Balsan, a dentist, bought fifty acres down the length of the St. Johns River at Yellow Bluff. He called the newly christened fishing village New Berlin after the city where he was born. According to Lauren Mosley, archivist of the Jacksonville Historic Society, New Berlin originally was designed as a community for mixed race descendants of wealthy slave owners. White people moved to New Berlin also. The town was segregated, but everyone socialized. By the late nineteenth century, there were about 100 people living at New Berlin. There were stores, churches, a post office, and the New Berlin Cemetery. As evidenced by the gravestone markers, families lived there for generations.

After a hardscrabble life, Napoleon began working for Captain David Kemp, a ship builder and a boat owner. He also fell in love with Captain Dave's beautiful daughter, Georgiana Carolinas Kemp. Whether she was called Georgie, the first name inscribed on her headstone, or Carrie, as most biographers claim, is unclear. What is clear is that shortly after Broward's sister, Josephine, died, the newlyweds moved into her house in Jacksonville. Alas, Georgiana soon contracted dengue fever, a mosquito-borne virus accompanied by a high fever, joint pain, and a rash. She gave birth to a baby boy, and they both died.

Napoleon Bonaparte Broward went on to become a sheriff, a governor, and finally a shoo-in for senator of Florida. He died of complications from gallstones before he could take office, twenty-seven years after the death of Georgiana. His infant namesake was the only son he ever sired; his second wife, Annie, bore him nine girls.

The *Miami News* lauded Broward in his obituary as "one of the greatest men the nation has ever produced" and "a man with an idea who fought for it while others jeered and laughed." The last tribute, of course, referred to his plan to "drain the Everglades" a controversial undertaking then and now. Marjorie Stoneman Douglas, Everglades champion and author of *The Everglades: River of Grass* accused Broward of irretrievably altering the Everglades with his dredging. Others lauded his efforts, his obituary notice declaring, "If a man is great who makes two blades of grass grow where one formerly grew, how much greater is the man who makes orchards and gardens possible where there was formerly nothing of use to man?" Unfortunately, in the bustling early part of the twentieth century, "nothing of use to man" included wildlife, flora, fauna, and the natural tributaries of Florida.

Regardless, the New Berlin cemetery is the historic resting place for the first family of a famous Florida leader. According to archives compiled by local historians Jan Smith and Betty Bleshoy, over 210 headstones stand in New Berlin Cemetery, the earliest dating to 1854 when Leonard Freeland expired at forty-four years of age. It is an eclectic cemetery, for those who care about such things, containing the graves of Masons, commercial fishermen, and veterans from many wars: Spanish-American, WWI, WWII, Korean, and Vietnam.

The state calls New Berlin an "enclave," which protects what's left of it from commercial development. Although funerals still occur at New Berlin Cemetery, the site itself is an obscure spot, and New Berlin residents seem to like it that way. It is the kind of cemetery that is hard to find. Like water flowing downhill, it finds you, instead.

Visitor Information

New Berlin Cemetery
Heckscher Drive
Jacksonville, FL 32226

Access is available at the end of Olympia Avenue off New Berlin Road and across the street from Yellow Bluff Fort.

Chapter 8

The Casa Marina Hotel

The saddest thing that I can imagine is to get used to luxury.
—**Charlie Chaplin**
Forbes, Inc. 1918

The Haunting

At one time, it was the host of Hollywood, but now it's Jacksonville Beach's best-kept secret. Its brochure says the Casa Marina Hotel is "a Grand Old Lady" and still turning heads at eighty. In fact, the hotel is ninety years old, and a precious hideaway amidst a boarded-up train depot and a near-deserted single-lane street. Go to the end of the dead end and there it is: the concrete and stucco Spanish Mediterranean revival-style hotel with the magnificent forest-green awning emblazoned with the distinctive initials CM.

Finding the Casa Marina Hotel is almost like running into a movie star on a public sidewalk. Staying at the Casa Marina Hotel, off-season anyway, is like an architectural embodiment of the ghost of Norma Desmond. Still beautiful, viable, and available, there is nonetheless, a sense of desolation and abandonment in the empty parking lot and the quiet halls of the once-grand hotel.

There are ghost stories associated with the hotel—flighty and unsubstantial: a seventh step on a stairwell where everyone trips, sightings of long-dead movie stars on the beaches, some pictures falling down, a few strange sounds.

At certain times of the year, there is a lone desk clerk for check in, and no guests. Up a few flights of stairs (past the haunted seventh step with no incident) to the Penthouse Lounge, the employees seemed startled to see customers. In the rooms, a red message light on the phone may flash with vintage voice mails from long-departed guests: Laura to Monica. Apparently, there was some party…

The skeleton staff isn't fool enough to put up a guest in the notorious room 206.

Guests get the ghost story from Sterling Joyce, a tall, handsome man of indeterminate age, who serves as the hotel's maître d' and event planner—

mostly weddings, although he did host Nike® for the Super Bowl and spent a day with Bill Crosby for some charity event. Apparently, the desolation of the hotel occurs during the post-New Year's lag.

Joyce has lived in Jacksonville for forty-five years and worked at the Casa Marina for seven. He knows the hotel and refers to events in terms of hotel rooms. Room 201 is "the jungle room" with the view of the ocean and the courtyard. Two years ago, Bill Cosby stayed in room 104. Room 103 was the room where the tourist family, who arrived in an RV, had to pack up and leave because the little girl kept hollering for her mother, declaring, "She' won't let me go to sleep." Who "she" was is undetermined, but another guest, during

The notorious and haunted room 206 and the hallway where a young bride ran to her death.

a wedding reception, asked Joyce, "Do you have ghosts?" Joyce shrugged. She whispered, "I've seen a little girl..."

Upstairs there is a panoramic view of the ocean and the beach. Joyce says the windows in the Penthouse Lounge unlock themselves. "We'd lock the windows. Every day they'd be unlocked. We put nails in them. They were still raised a little bit."

CM

The Casa Marina Hotel in Jacksonville Beach.

All of this leads up to the main ghost story, which concerns room 206. It happened in the 1930s when a newly married couple booked the notorious room. Sometime during the night, the man woke up alone. He began wandering through the hotel, in his striped pajamas, looking for his bride. It was summer, and, as Joyce explains it, the doors to the rooms were kept open to circulate the air in the absence of modern air conditioning.

The groom found his bride in room 212 with another man. The door was open, and he saw everything. He went back to room 206 and hung himself. His wife returned to find him dead.

"We used to have a small balcony at the end of the hallway," Joyce said. "She jumped off the balcony."

"It was only the second floor," a guest pointed out.

"Yeah, well, she died," Joyce said. "People say they still hear her running down the hall."

The History

Built in 1924, the Casa Marina Hotel was the most modern and fashionable hotel of its time. Constructed of stucco, tile, and concrete, the hotel had a newfangled fireproof sprinkler system activated by a water tower. Although there was no central air or heat, and guests had to share a bathroom, there were fine touches, such as the ceiling in the dining room of the Penthouse Lounge made from cypress taken from salvaged ships in the Atlantic Ocean. The original iron fence with spikes still divides the hotel from the dunes and the unparalleled view of Jacksonville Beach.

The sixty-room hotel is now divided into twenty-three "suites," all uniquely decorated with wooden floors, antique carved furniture, brass lamps, and marble and mosaic tile in the bathroom. Every room is different. The Jungle Room is laid with Indian print rugs on real wooden floors, which complement the textured walls, painted sea-foam green where oil paintings hang in gilt frames. The light fixtures are ornate and the "living room" features a fold-out couch, two comfy chairs, throw pillows, a mini-fridge and an extra TV stanchioned to the wall. Beyond the thick, green drapes and the wooden blinds, the Jungle Room has three windows facing the courtyard and the beach. There is a view of a dock leading to crinkled sand, a cluster of gulls, and the pinkish lapping waves of a sunrise, filling the room with mellow golden light. A lone jogger sprints barefoot in the sand past the hotel at dawn every day.

How many sunrises were shared by the likes of Jean Harlow, Fatty Arbuckle, Oliver Hardy, the Duke and Duchess of Windsor, or Charlie Chaplin? All of these epochal people may have occupied the Jungle Room.

Such notoriety drew the infamous as well. From their windows, silent film stars may have searched the horizon for Al Capone's yacht sailing up from Miami to provide hooch for their parties in the Prohibition era.

Prior to the 1920s, the white sands of Jacksonville's unnamed barrier island were known as Pablo Beach, named after the San Pablo River. On the day that the Casa Marina Hotel opened, the beachside community was rechristened "Jacksonville Beach."

Unofficially, the beach town was known as East Hollywood. Thousands of silent movies were filmed in the Jacksonville area while the stars partied at the Casa Marina. In fact, the partying and the disruption of the movie sets unsettled residents to the point where they elected a mayor who promised to make it clear to the movie studios that they were no longer welcome on Florida grounds. The studios and their stars took the hint and decamped for southern California. Unfortunately, within a decade, the Great Depression settled over the island.

Like so many of the grand hotels in the 1930s, business dwindled at the Casa Marina. During World War II, the government appropriated its sixty rooms for military housing. Then it was divided up into apartments. The hotel closed in the early '90s and the "grand old lady" was boarded up for eleven years.

Today, Sterling Joyce, the maitre d', insists business is good. He claims the beach is particularly popular for weddings. "We have five weddings in one weekend," Joyce said. "Three in one day. On 11-11-11 [November 11, 2011], the whole beach was loaded."

All is not fun and games, however. As the Casa Marina Hotel has seen its rise, its decline, and settled into its rarified existence as a best-kept secret on Jacksonville Beach, these are still hard times for a lot of people. Every year on December 14, his birthday, Joyce hosts a party for the needy. The owner turns the whole hotel over to him, and guests donate canned goods, food, and toys. "Last year, over 600 people came," Joyce said. "My charity is called Beaches Emergency Assistance Ministry (BEAM)."

It's a nice gesture for an employee from a luxury hotel with a big history and a select clientele. This may or may not include ghosts.

Visitor Information

The Casa Marina Hotel
691 N. 1st Street
Jacksonville Beach, FL 32250
http://casamarinahotel.com

Chapter 9

THE HOMESTEAD RESTAURANT

Dreams have only one owner at a time. That's why dreamers are lonely.

—Erma Bombeck
If Life is a Bowl of Cherries, What am I Doing in the Pits?

The Haunting

Anyone checking out the Homestead Restaurant on the Internet will find that it is closed for good. Driving down Beach Boulevard, in Jacksonville Beach, tourists often find the restaurant opened under another name. From 2011–2012, it was The Copper Top Restaurant. Today, it's a Mexican joint called TacoLu.

This was the restaurant where the ghosts of lonely old women reigned; in particular, the former proprietor, Alpha O. Paynter, who liked to materialize at the top of the stairs and in the background of mirrors. The restaurant is small; the adjoining "coppertop" bar is larger, but nearly empty, its orangey counter surface gleaming and devoid of glasses, ashtrays, and the lifting and the dropping of hands in expressive drunken gestures. Loud country, rock, and bluegrass used to play and there was karaoke. Former hostess Nicole Yousefzadeh, formerly of the Crab Cake Factory and of St. Augustine, a "consultant" who also kind of ran the place, knew a lot of the ghost stories. She said the restaurant was featured on a TV show, *Local Haunts*.

> *"Weird stuff, real weird stuff," Nicole said. "But I try to justify everything. I shut the TVs off, go upstairs, come down, and all the TVs are on. Lights go on that I know I turned off."*

This was all standard spook stuff. Nicole said abruptly, "Someone pulled my chair out from under me when I was sitting at the bar. There wasn't anyone behind me."

Clearly, she was warming up to something.

The Coppertop Bar in the former Homestead Restaurant.

> *Servers would say they'd come in and dishes would be all over the floor. Or the chairs would be flipped. Steve Macri? The former owner? He sat down with us when we opened and told us a bunch of stories. He had these two guys, migrants, working in the kitchen. Steve paid for a slab of concrete out back so they could play basketball. So the three of them were playing basketball. The ball went into the woods. One of the guys went after it, into the woods. He ran back out of the woods, crossed the street, and never came back. Steve called a week later and asked, "Do you want your check?" His mom answered. "No, he's never coming back. When he went into the woods, he saw a lady half in, half out of her grave."*

This story jibes with rumors that someone is buried in the land behind the restaurant. Whoever it is, it's not Alpha O. Paynter. According to her obituary, published in 1962, she died in nearby Neptune Beach, and she was cremated. Her ashy remains are nowhere near the restaurant. There are also stories about two other female proprietors who hung themselves in a storage closet; one in the 1960s, the other in the 1970s. It is unlikely, however, that someone buried them in the woods like a dead cat.

Yet, according to Nicole, there really is a Woman in White, an old lady, at the top of the stairs. Walking back and forth. Lots of people have seen her standing there, or as a reflection in the mirror. The haunting mostly take place in an old section of the restaurant, by the lime-rock fireplace, in the Ladies room, or on the second floor.

There used to be a ghost story printed on the menu about the first owner, Alpha O. Paynter: A very kind spirit, she is said to be simply still trying to look after the place and all its guests.

Does that sound like someone who would pull the chair out from under you? As far as restaurant ghost stories are concerned, season this one with a few grains of skeptical salt.

The History

The TacoLu Restaurant is just a two-story pine log cabin built in 1932, but the property is still enormously pricey, worth over 1.5 million dollars. (One of the former owners, Abbas Bagher, sold it for 2.2 million in 2006, although it closed again four years later.) It takes a lot of tacos to pay the property taxes on a place like that. The log cabin itself has cost more money than it's worth; the floors started sinking and buckling in 1994, so the restaurant closed for a month to install expensive concrete footers.

Before it went through a string of owners, opening and closing periodically, like a clam on construction prone Beach Boulevard, TacoLu was a boarding house, sitting on an eighteenth century land grant acquired from a Spaniard, De Castro Y Ferrer. Alpha O. Paynter turned the boarding house into a restaurant, and her fried chicken recipe into a "food tradition."

Beach residents grew up eating fried chicken at the Homestead. A popular dish, it came with sides of biscuits, rice, coleslaw, and macaroni and cheese. In the 1990s, the restaurant went through close to 4,000 pounds of chicken in a week, feeding the tantalizing dish to 300 customers a night. They also squished into the adjoining Copper Top Bar, once known as a "skinny bar." According to Nicole:

> *It was only yea big. People had to pile in together. There was a barber chair where everyone took shots.*

Whether TacoLu, serving Mexican cuisine, will catch on is anyone's guess. The restaurant hasn't really been successful since its original inception, despite a slew of owners.

One could say that Alpha O. Paynter is not going to rest in peace until TacoLu gets fired up.

Maybe that's why she's still jostling chairs.

Visitor Information

The TacoLu Restaurant
1712 Beach Boulevard
Jacksonville Beach, FL 32250
http://tacolu.com/

Chapter 10

GINGER'S PLACE

An intelligent man is sometimes forced to be drunk, to spend time with his fools.

—Ernest Hemingway
For Whom the Bell Tolls

The Haunting

Four and a half blocks from Jacksonville beach, Ginger's Place is just a bar across the street from a Taco Bell. Except for the painted windows with the silhouettes of women on the second floor, it's a nondescript hole-in-the wall with an air conditioning wall unit, a jukebox, and a clientele that goes back to the 1960s. One of the regulars, Randy, sits on a bar stool, smokes a cigarette, and tells no one in particular about his first foray as a callow Navy recruit:

It used to be a biker joint called The Glass Bar. I came in my uniform, looked around, saw the leather and chains, and turned to go. One guy hollered at me, "Where you going [expletive]?"

Randy told him he didn't think it was his kind of a bar.

The biker replied, "Get in here, [expletive]." So, he did. The biker dude told him, "You're serving my country, and I want to buy you a drink." Randy takes a long drag on his cigarette. "They turned out to be the nicest fellas. I went there for a month and never spent a dime. Went overseas and came back—it was a dress shop by then. But it's been Ginger's Place for thirty-five years."

He pauses, looks around, and inclines his head confidentially."It's haunted," he whispers.

Randy has lived in the Jacksonville Beach area all his life, and he looks like a steady guy, out for a beer on a Friday night, not someone prone to flights of fancy. Sitting at the bar, he points to a small rectangular opening dividing the kitchen from the drinking area.

Ginger's Place in Jacksonville Beach.

"People see people in the kitchen when there's no one there," he says.

"Who do they see?" someone asks.

"Some woman."

"Have you ever seen anything?"

Randy turns earnest and starts rattling off events. "The sign "Women" flew off the door of the restroom and landed near the drums." He waves a hand at the restrooms in the corner of the bar and the band instruments set up against the wall in the center of the room.

"His audience is unimpressed."

"Is that it?"

"Nope. One day? I was sitting here with Jamal [the bartender]. No one was here but us. Someone banged my chair hard. Another guy, he felt a hand brush over his hair."

Jamal, a five-year employee of Ginger's, who doubles as a bartender and a bouncer, chimes in. "See these glass shelves?" he asks, gesturing toward the row of glasses above the liquor bottles. "They slanted and all the glasses stayed in place. Not one thing broke."

Is it unusual for grown men with jobs to be talking about eerie events, rather than about sports or women? Jamal had one more story. "I was working the door. And I was standing outside. And I heard a voice say, 'Get inside.' And I went in just in time to break up what woulda been a very bad fight. Three guys on each side."

Who warned Jamal?

According to various news reports featuring Samantha Robenolt, it's her grandmother, Darlene "Ginger" Parsons, the former proprietor, former Vaudeville performer, former stripper, and the former star of an underwater mermaid show. Ginger was a quirky woman who was fond of unusual monikers as evidenced by her late husband "Ziggy" and by her daughters "Taffy" and "Candy."

Other people have seen Ginger floating around. An article in the *Florida Times-Union* in 2010, by Maggie FitzRoy, details the experience of a disk jockey who saw a woman with curly-blonde hair literally walk through the kitchen door.

Robenolt said her grandma, Ginger, had curly blonde hair.

The glass shelf behind the bar at Ginger's Place. It collapsed, but nothing broke.

The History

According to Duval County Records, Ginger and Ziggy bought the property on South 3rd Street in 1977. It was nothing special: just a bar under 1,400 square feet with no air conditioning. Ginger put pictures of herself up on the walls and arranged mannequins, dressed in her clothes, in provocative poses in the upstairs windows. Ginger's Place became a neighborhood bar where all the locals hung out, listened to music, or made requests of disc jockeys spinning disks on the weekend.

Ginger continued to run the bar after Ziggy died in the late '80s. In the spring of 2003, she spent a month in a nursing home, and by December, she was dead. Ginger left the place to her daughters Candy and Taffy, although it wasn't worth much more than it was when Ginger and Ziggy bought it in the late '70s. The daughters renovated the bar in 2004, which according to granddaughter Samantha, is when the paranormal sightings began.

Samantha was so concerned, she even brought in some ghost hunters, the Paranormal Outcast Investigations (P.O.I) to verify the presence of Ginger. The P.O.I's findings were inconclusive, although they documented "strange feelings" and "a few unexplained noises." However, that can't be an unusual occurrence after a night of drinking at any bar.

Some people may think, like Randy on that long ago night when he walked in the door for the first time, that Ginger's isn't their kind of place. They're wrong. Ginger's Place is the opposite extreme of, say, the Penthouse Lounge at the Casa Marina Hotel, which is down the street, with its cypress walls and its view of the ocean. Ginger's is cramped, cluttered, and when patrons look out the front door, all they see is Beach Boulevard and a fast-food joint. But sometimes you don't feel like dressing up and, on those occasions, it's Ginger's for the locals.

Whether Ginger haunts the place or not, her bar is the last of a smoky, cluttered, noisy breed; the neighborhood bar where people unwind and everyone knows your name.

Visitor Information

Ginger's Place
304 3rd Street South
Jacksonville Beach, FL 32250

Chapter 11

Singleton's Seafood Shack

My husband was born on a houseboat on the St. Johns River. He was on the water all his life.

—Ann Singleton
From *Florida, A Journey Through Its Colorful Past*
by Patty DiRienzo

The Haunting

Perched on the very brink of the old Mayport Village in Duval County, Singleton's Seafood Shack presides over the St. Johns River and a parking lot full of cars and feral cats. It is a weathered property with a porch built up on pilings over the water, where pelicans glide overhead and ducks swim underneath. Through the humble walkway is a posted sign: *Friends don't let friends eat imported shrimp.* Inside, patrons can see how fresh the seafood is because it accumulates, raw, in an iced trough by the entrance.

Tourists take the ferry over from Fort George Island. When the restaurant isn't busy, the waitress sits a party of four on a long L-shaped picnic-style table. The menus feature items such as "Minorcan clam chowder."

Most orders consist of variations of famous Mayport shrimp. If she's in the mood, the waitress will tell you that the shack is haunted. "The lights go on and off," she'll say, scribbling on her order pad. "Whiskey bottles move around on their own. I was a little freaked out at first, but now I'm used to it.'

On Saturday nights, the place is busy. Larry, a guy who drives over on weekends from Jacksonville, tells tourists that the entire town is built over a sixteenth century Spanish graveyard.

If that isn't good enough, Larry points to a wall of newspaper clippings. The news items are about the former owner of the seafood shack, Captain Ray Singleton.

Captain Ray worked on the water and lived in Mayport all of his life, except for a four-year "stint on an aircraft carrier during World War II." This was a guy who started working when he was fourteen, who swabbed the decks of charter boats and who learned the trade of shrimping before he could drive. He had

Shrimp boats docked in the old Mayport Village.

diabetes, though, and he eventually lost a leg to it. He didn't get around as much anymore. Suddenly, his focus changed.

In the back of Singleton's Seafood Shack is a museum. Actually, it's just a room with dozens of model boats built of wood, displayed casually, perched on a dining room table and on any other flat surface. The boats range in size from a foot to several yards. They're made of mahogany, poplar, and cedar. This is Captain Ray's boatbuilding museum. Some of the model boats are painted, but most are not. The painted ones have names hand lettered on their hulls. One is "Miss Ann" the name of Captain Ray's wife.

He began building model boats to scale, strictly from memory, without photographs or blueprints, when he was a teenager. In the last years of his life, he built dozens of miniature crafts, from shrimp boats to tugboats to all of the major vessels in the St. Johns River and the Atlantic canal waters of northeastern Florida.

There are over 100 model boats and he kept them all, displaying them in his restaurant. A painted shrimp boat, completely outfitted with nets, is mounted near the entrance. Captain Singleton christened it "Ray's Pride."

His model boats landed him the Florida Folk Heritage Award in 1991, signed by Governor Lawton Chiles. The award is still displayed in the restaurant, with all the clippings, although Captain Ray himself is long gone; he died of cancer in 1997.

There is a picture of the old man displayed as well. Captain Ray poses next to a model shrimp boat in suspender and shirtsleeves, smoking a cigarette. He's a white-haired guy with a beard, missing teeth, and sporting a tat on his forearm. He loved his model boats too much to sell them, although he'd had offers, and he loved to tell stories about his boats, and his life. The little museum in the back features other artifacts as well. There are pictures of shrimp boats, a life-sized plaster shark with a bottle of Captain Morgan® in its jaws, old motors, and a baseball trophy.

Does Captain Ray haunt Singleton's Seafood Shack? Of that, no one knows. But it is rare to enter a seafood dive and find artifacts worthy of a museum, crafts built so intuitively and with such care and detail, that the nautical executor of their maritime design is, seriously, an almost palpable presence.

The History

Singleton's Seafood Shack is a family restaurant, and it's been that way for generations. Captain Ray's grandmother called it Aunt Sally's and dished up burgers and hot dogs. Captain Ray and his wife, Miss Ann, converted it as a seafood market and then into a popular seafood restaurant. Singleton's son, Dean, runs the restaurant today with help from Miss Ann, who is alive albeit wheelchair bound.

From Fort George Island, tourists can see the Mayport restaurant across the St. Johns River. To get there, drive the car aboard the St. Johns River ferryboat, park it, and watch the pelicans congregate and glide overhead as the ferry cruises over the water to Mayport Village, founded in 1562 when the famous French Huguenot, Jean Ribault landed in the harbor. The restaurant is one block from the ferry on A1A.

A road divides the Mayport Naval base and the restaurant. Down that road is a registered National Historic Lighthouse. It stands behind a fence of barbed wire and asphalt. Not far away, a memorial marker on the side of the road narrates the likelihood of a sixteenth century Spanish graveyard lying below Broad Street. There was talk about the Navy helping the Mayport locals to find out more about the cemetery, to protect it and to register it as a national historic site. They did put the memorial marker up, noting that a permit was required to disturb the soil, and noting that the cemetery was, in fact, on navy property just like the St. Johns lighthouse.

Further restoration plans may have been lost to the town's intermittent hysteria, which accompanies the snooping of the Jacksonville Port Authority

Captain Ray's model boats.

around the fishing village to determine whether to build a Carnival cruise ship terminal in Mayport's deep harbor. Jaxport found a port somewhere else, but the behemoth Carnival Fascination cruises pass Singleton's twice a day. Tourists, not locals, turn out of the restaurant to watch it glide by. They wave.

Regardless, the plywood seafood shack with the hand-lettered sign abides, still crowded with locals and Jacksonville residents on a Saturday night. Everyone sits around cypress tables, under hanging lamps with beer logos, framed by windows hung with fishnet and buoy curtains, eating shrimp, squid, gator tail, oysters, mahi-mahi, clams, conch fritters, slaw, collard greens, and hush puppies off Styrofoam plates with plastic utensils. There is a big ship steering wheel in the dining room, and T-shirts are for sale behind the bar. The seafood is great and the atmosphere is Old Florida.

And, of course, there are the model boats and Captain Ray's boatbuilding museum in the back, clear evidence of how much Captain Ray loved the water that he lived on all his life. Perhaps he found it hard to leave when life ended.

Visitor Information

Singleton's Seafood Shack
4728 Ocean Street
Mayport, FL 32233

Pelicans on pilings near the St. Johns River ferryboat.

NASSAU COUNTY

Chapter 12

The Addison on Amelia Island

Who among your neighbors would be around 100 years hence, haunting the old neighborhood?

—From the file on
The Addison in the Amelia Island Museum of History
Author Unknown

The Haunting

Told by Amelia Island Museum of History volunteer docent Steve Sansbury:

Thea [Seagraves], our volunteer coordinator has seen this phenomena many times with the previous owners. We call it the "Goldilocks Story."

You see this second floor and the room at the middle end of it? When you tidy up a bed and breakfast, or any hotel room, the first thing you do is clean the room, put fresh linens on the bed, open the curtains and let some light in, shut the door and lock it. Guests would come into this room, right here, and come downstairs and say, "Someone has been sleeping in my bed." There was a perfect impression of a human being in the middle of the bed, like he'd been lying there sleeping. The door would still be locked.

The interesting thing was that the curtains would be drawn. So it was dark in there. They never caught anyone doing it, but the owners would call Thea and say, "Quick, come see it, he's done it again."

The History

The oldest part of the pistachio green Addison House Bed and Breakfast was built in 1876 in the Greek Revival style. Frank Simmons, a news dealer on Centre Street, owned it. He lived across the street, from Kate and Effingham Bailey, and the Baileys actually stayed with the Simmons while their house was being built. Bailey and Simmons also collaborated in a streetcar business, and they made sure the stops included their homes. This caused trouble within Bailey's marriage (see Chapter 15: The Bailey House).

The Addison Bed and Breakfast House on Amelia Island.

The original Addison kitchen was outside the main house and linked by a roofed passageway with open sides. Then for the decade between 1970 and 1980, the house was converted into apartments. Named after a former owner's daughter, today the spacious bed and breakfast has expanded to over 8,000 square feet, incorporating fifteen suites. That includes the two newer buildings built in the late 1990s, a common courtyard with a three-layered fountain, and fifteen and half bathrooms.

The house has always been distinctive for its two-story chimney, its gabled porch, gingerbread trim, and wooden columns. Made of wood frame and roofed with metal shingles over eleven foot high ceilings, it is a certified historic property registered with the Historic District Council. As such, the interior features heart-of-pine floors and original doors, plaster molding, and five decorative fireplaces and mantels. All fifteen rooms are decorated Florida style: pastels, wicker, and floral prints. Many of the rooms feature four-poster beds.

The central staircase is a relic from the famous Egmont Hotel, Florida's first big tourist hotel built in 1877. In fact, the Addison stands across the street from another famous building, the Tabby House (the only house on Amelia Island constructed entirely out of oyster shell, limestone, and sand).

The original owner, Simmons, was a good neighbor, and his amicable nature would clearly approve of his home's present status as a popular bed and breakfast. Who sleeps in the bed in the old section of the house is anyone's guess.

Perhaps his old friend and business partner, Effingham Bailey, still in trouble with Kate, is spending one more night.

Visitor Information

Addison on Amelia Island
614 Ash Street
Amelia Island, FL 32034
www.addisononamelia.com

Chapter 13

Amelia Island Paint and Hardware Store

But what is Hope? Nothing but the paint on the face of Existence; the least touch of truth rubs it off, and then we see what a hollow-cheeked harlot we have got hold of.

—Lord Byron
Letters and Journals of Lord Byron

The Haunting

Told by Amelia Island Museum of History Volunteer docent Penny Sansbury:

Back when Fernandina was in its heyday, before the Civil War, this was Spanish territory. Of course, Fernandina has a natural harbor with very deep water. So this was the perfect place for pirates and soldiers to come ashore. There were more bordellos here than there were restaurants and bars, and every bar was connected to a bordello. In fact, Ladies Street in Old Town was not named for conventional "ladies."

There were separate bars for the workers on the ships, the enlisted men, than there were for the officers. When the Palace Saloon was started, it was for the officers. This building was for the enlisted men.

The young man who works here says if he's there at night, working on the books, he can hear parties, music, people laughing, glasses clinking. The people who live around here have seen a woman come out in a fancy dress in the middle of the night; they try to take a picture, and the woman disappears. There's one apparition in particular, a lady in red, that they've seen here and coming out of another building over on Centre Street.

The History

The Amelia Island Paint and Hardware Store, built in 1876, has infamous origins. After its stint as a house of ill repute, it functioned as a grocery store until the 1980s, when Georgia native and Merchant Marine vet Ralph Palmisano got into the paint business. Right away, the concrete block corner

The Amelia Island Paint and Hardware Store near downtown Fernandina Beach.

store was a gathering place for locals to swap news, gossip, and tips for home repairs.

Ralph forged friendships within the community, calling every customer by name, and serving snacks in the afternoons. He expanded Amelia Island Paints into Amelia Island Paint and Hardware throughout the ensuing decade, although to the locals, the store was "Ralph's." He was generous, but he was a businessman and no pushover; if customers didn't pay their bills, they landed in court. The Palmisanos prospered, and Ralph owned the paint and hardware store free and clear by the 1990s. When Ralph died of lung cancer in 2003, his son, Andy, took over the business.

The Amelia Island Paint and Hardware Store is not a behemoth retail wasteland. Instead, it is exactly the kind of generational mom-and-pop establishment that is fast disappearing from the American business landscape. A cultural as well as an historical icon, it is still an establishment that caters to the working man and woman, although its current clientele no longer features pirates, soldiers, and ladies with bad reputations. In fact, modern customers are a vast improvement, including owners of local bed and breakfast inns, tourists, retirees, and merchants who, if they still want to "paint the town red," mean it literally, not figuratively.

Visitor Information

Amelia Island Paint and Hardware Store
516 Ash Street
Fernandina Beach, FL 32034

Chapter 14

Amelia Island Williams House

Never be haughty to the humble or humble to the haughty.
—Jefferson Davis

The Haunting

When the Spanish sold Florida to the United States in 1821, they wanted to know how much land they actually had. They hired Marcellus Williams to do the survey; he also did all the surveying in the Miami and the Everglades areas.

The wood-frame two-story antebellum house on South 9th Street, where Williams lived, is a bed and breakfast inn now. According to Steve Sansbury, a volunteer docent for the Amelia Island Museum of History, it was during a shoot for a promotional brochure in the parlor that a picture developed with a blurry image of a man in the parlor mirror.

Since then, other people have seen a man sitting in a chair, smoking a pipe, and wearing a funny little hat. In the nineteenth century, many professions had their own hats, like the striped engineer's hat. The hat described in the Williams' house, based on pictures of a surveyor's cap, is the same hat that the ghost wears. Marcellus Williams reportedly died in a chair in that location of the house in 1912.

In the front of the Williams house, there's a beautiful central staircase with the parlor on one side and the dining room on the other. In the dining room, a cabinet that used to be a china closet has a back-bottom panel that pushes out. Pulled away from the wall, the cabinet hides a little room, a secret room, created under the house. Historians think it's one of the early hiding places for the Underground Railroad, an organization that smuggled slaves out of the South before and during the Civil War.

Williams was from an old Southern family, and he actually entertained Jefferson Davis, and stored some of the Confederate president's furniture and belongings in his own home. Why was he, of all people, smuggling slaves up north?

And why does he keep returning?

The William's House Bed and Breakfast on Amelia Island.

The History

The city of Fernandina is a series of Spanish land grants acquired by ship captain and plantation owner Domingo Fernandez in the early nineteenth century. In 1821, his heirs sold the land to David Yulee, president of the Florida Railroad Company and the first United States senator from Florida. He, in turn, broke the land up and sold it.

In the mid-nineteenth century, a Boston banker built the house on South 9th Street in the Greek Revival style. He wanted "no expense spared," so the 5,000-square-foot house was constructed of brick and heart pine with a gable roof, and thirteen foot floor-to-ceiling windows. There is a distinctive "one of a kind" gingerbread design on the verandahs. There were six fireplaces, four of which were of hand-carved mahogany. The original iron fence still stands today.

Yet, the Yankee banker, an enemy of secession, couldn't abide the South, so he sold in less than a year. The buyer was Marcellus Williams, an illustrious surveyor and the owner of a huge amount of woodlands in Nassau County.

Williams married a Mayport heiress, the great-great granddaughter of the king of Spain. They settled in Fernandina because of its large Spanish community. He planted the huge oaks along Ash and 9th for shade and for her comfort. Yet, in addition to being a successful businessman and a devoted husband and father (the Williams had nine children), Williams was also a canny man of conscience.

In spite of his overt friendship with the Confederate president, Williams freed his slaves prior to the Civil War. He moved his family to Volusia County during the war, while he became active in the Underground Railroad. His home in Fernandina was known as a "safe house" for runaway slaves.

Not everyone appreciated his bravery. In 1994, in a missive to a local magazine, a relative of the Williams family, Mrs. Jackie Hines, wrote: "The fact that Marcellus Williams was not a Confederate was very seldom mentioned and not something we were proud of."

The Williams family occupied the home for over a century, yet today it is a bed and breakfast with ten rooms furnished with exquisite antiques. *National Geographic Traveler's Magazine* reviews it as "...one of the top twenty-five inns in the south." It is advertised as a romantic getaway and its website contains gushing testimonials for the site where true love blossoms and wedding plans are laid. In fact, the Amelia Island Williams House offers a special "Vow Renewal" package for couples who want to get married all over again in front of twenty of their closest friends.

The Williams House is the former home of a brave man who surveyed life from a different perspective than the conventional wisdom of his peers. So if Marcellus Williams shows up in the photographs, don't be alarmed. If a Civil War hero who saved the lives and promoted the freedom of enslaved human beings isn't numbered among your closest friends...he'll keep coming back until he is.

Visitor Information

Amelia Island's Williams House
103 S. 9th Street
Amelia Island, FL 32034
http://williamshouse.com

Chapter 15

The Bailey House and Kate Bailey's Tree

I think that I shall never see a poem lovely as a tree.
—**Joyce Kilmer**
"Trees"

The Haunting

The best place to take pictures of the big oak tree on Ash Street is from the parking lot of a grocery store. A guy who pulled up in a truck, wearing a Lawn Service work shirt with gray hair that spiked out of the back of a RealTree ball cap, disavowed any knowledge of the tree:

> *That tree? There's a story attached to it. I don't know. I've lived here since I was three, and I'm fifty-eight years old. That tree has always been there.*

So, to the RealTree guy, here is the story you waited 55 years to hear:

As told by volunteer docent Steve Sansbury of the Amelia Island Museum of History:

> *The house was a wedding present from Effingham Bailey to his wife Kate Bailey. He told her, "Kate, we have a certain amount of money. I can build you a big house, but I can't furnish it. I can build you a small house, and we can furnish it right away. Which would you rather have?" Kate was a smart girl; she asked for the big house. They furnished it in about two years.*
>
> *This adjoining street here, Ash Street, used to be a single-lane road that ran all the way down to a pavilion on the beach. One morning, Kate was sitting on her porch in a rocking chair, and she looked up and there were all these men with measuring tools looking at the huge ancient oak tree growing in the middle of the unpaved street. She asked, "What are you doing?"*
>
> *The men said, "Miz Bailey, you're in luck. We're going to run a streetcar line right down this street. Gotta cut the tree down to put in the streetcar line." In those days, the wealthy were the ones on the streetcar lines.*
>
> *The next morning the men came back with their saws, and their axes, and their picks, and they looked up and Kate Bailey was sitting right there in front of the tree*

Kate Bailey's oak tree, which she defended with a shotgun.

with a shotgun in her lap. They looked at the shotgun and they decided, "We need somebody higher up." So, they went to their supervisor, who went to the city fathers. They all said, "Kate Bailey is defending that tree with a shotgun. We think she's crazy enough to shoot us over that tree."

The tree is still there.

That wasn't the end of the Bailey's interesting past, although some of it includes their afterlife. In recent years, the Bailey house has seen all kinds of apparitions. People have heard funeral music coming from the house when no one was home. They've seen a man in a gray suit walking through the house; Effingham Bailey often wore a gray suit. Kate Bailey died in the room upstairs and she has been seen since then looking out of that window. Her own granddaughter, Maria, described an icy chill upon mounting the steps to her room, and a feeling of dread that was so intense she had to be hospitalized.

The History

Not mentioned in the Kate Bailey tree legend is the fact that her husband Effingham Bailey collaborated with a neighbor on a streetcar business. So, it may have been Effingham Bailey, the husband of Kate, who initially put her beloved oak tree at risk.

Architect George Barber designed the house, which was built in 1895. Like many of the big, beautiful Victorian houses in Fernandina's historic district, the Old Bailey House once functioned as a bed and breakfast. Today the two-and-a-half-storied peach- and blue-shuttered house is listed on the National Register of Historic Sites and privately owned by George and Barbara Sheffield, who are also the owners of the Palace Saloon.

The Old Bailey House has nine bedrooms and 11.5 bathrooms. The exterior is quite imposing, featuring gables, turrets, windows of all dimensions, geometric corner towers, a type of unique scale-shingle, and a wraparound porch.

Even in today's housing market, the 7,000 square feet of property is worth close to a million dollars. The front porch is decorated with carousel horses, which were put up originally as Christmas decorations, but now remain outside year-round.

And, of course, Kate's oak tree, immense with age still stands smack in the middle of Ash Street, clearly visible from Old Bailey House. When Kate's specter appears in the window of her old room, perhaps she takes solace from the enduring legacy of her lovely tree.

Visitor Information

The Bailey House
28 South 7th Street
Fernandina Beach, FL 32034
www.nationalregisterofhistoricplaces.com/fl/Nassau/state.html

The Bailey House with its distinctive carousel of painted wooden horses.

Chapter 16

THE BOOK LOFT

Out, out brief candle.
—**William Shakespeare**
Macbeth

The Haunting

The Book Loft is a yellow two-story building with white shutters and a green awning on Centre Street, specializing in books by Florida writers and in signed, first editions, two aspects of collectibles that appeal to compulsive bookaphiles.

In mid-October, during a street festival featuring antique cars, the bookstore was hushed and cool with whitewashed brick walls, wooden bookshelves and fringed Indian rugs. Local author Maggie Carter-de Vries's book *Ghosts of Amelia & Other Tales* is prominently displayed on the dining room table. The cashier tells customers that The Book Loft is featured as a haunted site in de Vries's book. Cathy Schultz has worked at 214 Centre Street for eight years, and this is her ghost story:

One night I locked up, everything neat and orderly. I came in the next day and, upstairs? In the loft? There were two stacks of books. They were taller than five-feet-two inches, which is what I am. The stacks were neat and orderly and they were all the books from the top shelves.

Electric lights go on and off a lot. Some employees say they've seen a little girl in old-fashioned clothes. She doesn't speak. She looks sad.

When we took over, this was a gift shop and before that a millinery. In one of the back rooms, we found a picture of a young lady. From the late nineteenth, early twentieth century I'd say. We don't know who she is. We all have our suspicions.

There is a display of the framed sepia tinted picture. It is a head and shoulders shot of sad, melancholy eyes in an unsmiling face. The girl looks to be about twelve years old with brown wavy hair. She wears a white dress with a lace frill and a necklace—perhaps a St. Francis medal.

Although it is unlikely that the young girl in the picture is a neat and

The mysterious "girl in white" who haunts The Book Loft on Fernandina Beach's Centre Street.

orderly ghost given to eccentric book displays, paranormal ghost chasers speculate that poltergeist activity, of which stacking is a common outcome, is a type of telekinesis, or the power to move things through the force of will. It occurs most often around young girls on the brink of puberty who are experiencing some type of dysfunction, agitation, or turmoil. Could this theory apply to the mysterious spirit of the preteen in the picture on display at the Book Loft?

I can only say that when Bob looked through his camera lens, he saw a mysterious orb of light near the cash register that couldn't be accounted for by the electricity, the windows, or the passing cars (there were none, the street was closed). He shook his head, looked again, and the light was gone. It was a brief illumination, signifying...probably nothing. It still leaves plenty of room for speculation.

The History

The Book Loft's motto is Garrison Keillor's quote, "A book is a present you can open again and again."

Of course, that is true only if the book is preserved. Nearby Jacksonville and St. Augustine suffered their share of horrendous fires and Fernandina Beach on Amelia Island was no exception. After a fire leveled Centre Street in the late nineteenth century, the city passed a law that certainly enhanced Keillor's and the Book Loft's certainty. The law required brick for all building construction, and downtown Fernandina Beach is indeed a brick and mortar bastion in a small southern thoroughfare.

The thoroughfare itself is its main strip, Centre Street, an historic district over fifty blocks long and lined with hundreds of buildings, all listed on the National Register of Historic Places. In December, there's a holiday tour of historic homes where visitors can view the Victorian-era architecture up close and personally. Then they can buy a book about the island's history.

Unexplained glow of light among the book stacks.

"We call ourselves an old-fashioned bookstore," Cathy Schultz says. "Authors like it, too. John Grisham comes here to sign his books. So does Carl Hiaasen."

The downstairs features book displays on dining room tables and, in the front room, closest to the street, are a wall of bookshelves with the names of Florida writers on the binding. Up three steps, wooden railing guards the elevated shelves of signed, first editions. The back rooms are for the older books and the children's reading room. On top of all the wooden bookshelves are antiques: a manual typewriter, tennis rackets, black and white photographs of Amelia Island and prints by local artists, suitcases, a hatbox, a snow sled, and a bear in a top hat.

The loft, where the book stacking occurs, is to the right of the entrance and accessed via a staircase to the top floor. The top floor looks out on Centre Street through windows with flower boxes attached to windowsills. Although there are many bookshelves up there, too, there are also homey lamps, and a dining room table for reading, researching, and writing.

Built in 1900, The Book Loft is over 3,000 square feet; it was expanded in the 1970s and the awning was added in the 1990s. The same owner has held the mortgage for over twenty years.

Perhaps that is why book lovers feel a sense of relief within the walls of this low-key bookstore, with the homey touches, catering to a clientele who want something different from the latest *New York Times* blockbuster inside of a cookie cutter book mall. It is an old-fashioned source of commercial literature. One can almost picture the brown-haired girl in the sepia picture solemnly mounting the stairs to the loft, holding a candle to light her way.

Visitor Information

The Book Loft
214 Centre Street
Fernandina Beach, FL 32034

The Book Loft storefront on Centre Street.

Chapter 17

Bosque Bello Cemetery

The woods are lovely, dark, and deep.

—Robert Frost
"Stopping By Woods on a Snowy Evening"

The Haunting

Told by Amelia Island Museum of History volunteer docent Steve Sansbury:

There was a period on Amelia Island when there was really no law of the land, and a French pirate, Luis Aury, emerged. He was a mercenary. He eventually left Fernandina, but he didn't take everything with him. He left an illegitimate son who was as bad as his father, maybe worse.

His name was Luc Aury—he was a thief, a scoundrel, he assaulted women, and he beat up men. He was a terrible person. The town finally got tired of him. They said, "We are going to capture Luc Aury." They did, and then they took him to the jail. They said, "Tomorrow morning, at daylight, you're going to hang."

Well, the entire town, when they heard about it, turned out that night. It was literally a celebration; they thought it was wonderful. Well, Luc Aury...he did not want to hang. So he slashed his own throat with a razor. A doctor was summoned. They said, "Keep him alive until daylight." So the doctor sewed him up.

Sure enough, at daylight, he had a pulse. He was breathing. They had to lift him onto the gallows. They put a noose around his neck, held him up, and then they dropped him.

When they did, the stitches didn't hold. Luc was literally decapitated. Everyone was sprayed in blood. It was one of the most horrible sights ever seen in Fernandina. Children were literally run over by adults getting out of the way of this terrible sight. We don't know where he's buried; probably in Bosque Bello, although in those days they didn't mark the graves very well.

Over the years, people would tell you about this terrible sound they'd hear at Bosque Bello, this moaning sound. Some people said it was the wind; others said it could only be the sound of a man being hung and having his head pulled off.

Sunset view of the Bosque Bello Cemetery.

Main entrance to the cemetery and the oak tree where Luc Aury was decapitated in the nineteenth century.

The History

In the early 1800s, the French pirate, Luis Aury, Luc's father, actually reigned over Fernandina Beach for a short period and staked one of its eight flags: the rebel flag of the Mexican Revolution. Luis held no allegiance to Mexico or to any other sovereign state; it was the only flag handy, and Luis immediately commenced slave trading, bringing more than 1,000 slaves a month to Fernandina Beach. At that time, Fernandina was a haven for pirates and buried treasure. Rumors still circulate throughout the island about locations for gold doubloons. Within a year, however, the United States Navy ousted Luis from Fernandina.

Doubtless Luc Aury was conceived during his pirate father's brief administration as territorial pirate-in-chief. Most of the sources of the stories about Luis' illegitimate son Luc Aury agree that, after years of terrorizing the town, the profligate scoundrel was captured by Fernandina authorities and taken into custody where he slashed his own throat, and survived, only to be gruesomely decapitated during his hanging at daybreak. The stories differ only in the location of where he was hung.

De Vries, in her book *Ghosts of Amelia*, situates the event at the jail (now the Amelia Island Museum of History) on 3rd Street. Volunteer docent Sansbury pins the Luc Aury death near an ancient oak tree across the street from the current entrance to the Bosque Bello Cemetery on 14th Street. Thea Seagraves, volunteer coordinator of the museum, says that her volunteers tell both versions of the Luc Aury story, because the records are imprecise, and no one can be certain exactly where Aury lost his head.

Regardless, the Bosque Bello Cemetery is a quaint spot, off the beaten track, near Old Town, a hidden trove of history surrounded by a city that has grown up around it. From a high knoll, there is a view of the Amelia River surrounded by old oaks covered with Spanish moss and resurrection fern. Wandering around the uneven mounds of Bosque Bello, the "beautiful woods," visitors are always struck by the incongruous landscape of sun and shadows cast by ancient oaks and cedars, permeated, not by a sea breeze seasoned with magnolia, but with the visible belching malodorous smoke of pulp and paper mills. People in town call it, "the smell of money," but from the perspective of wandering around an old cemetery, it smells more like sulfur and brimstone. Bosque Bello may be beautiful, but it is also sinister.

Its origins, however, are benign and altruistic. Domingo Fernandez, holder of the Spanish land grant, donated the land for the free cemetery in the old section in 1798. At that time, the Bosque Bello entrance opened off 8th Street onto unpaved lanes—Magnolia, Oleander, Redbud—that still crisscross the property. It is a nonsectarian cemetery, although, like everything else in antebellum Florida, the old section is segregated by race; blacks are buried in the old enclave on the north side.

The Nassau County Genealogical Society has meticulously documented grave records, but there are still many unknowns about Bosque Bello's interred population. Historian Alice Youngblood wrote in her 1937 "History of Fernandina" that a Bosque Bello sexton revealed to her that he often unearthed unidentified human bones whenever he dug a new grave.

The oldest identifiable grave at the cemetery dates from 1813: Peter Bouissou de Nicar, who is listed as a "French Soldier" on the Nassau County Genealogy and History website for Bosque Bello Cemetery. Youngblood wrote that de Nicar was, in fact, more of a mercenary. Buried next to him is Father Patrick Halligan, who in 1963 asked to be buried next to a "reprobate" after the priest fell out of favor with the bishop.

The rest of the Fernandina citizens in the old section rest in peace under the slightly rolling land covered with looming moss-covered live oak. There are a limited number of early monuments because all of the stone markers were imported; no native local stone was used. Traditionally, women were buried to the left of the men, and the graves faced east, so that when the resurrected sat up during the Rapture, they would have a clear view of their Lord.

Grave markers of union soldiers from Fort Clinch.

These lucky internments include a former lighthouse keeper, Amos Latham, who fought in the Revolutionary War, Confederate and Union soldiers, soldiers of the Spanish American War, and some of the former Fernandina citizens who star in local ghost stories. These include: Major Thomas Leddy of the Florida House Inn (Chapter 18), Major Ferdinand Charles Suhrer, shot on the steps of an inn by Thomas Eppes (Chapter 27), and Mother Celenie and Sister de Sales, who were moved from the churchyard after they died of yellow fever during the epidemic in 1877 (Chapter 24). Any grave in Bosque Bello with a death date of 1877 marks the remains of a yellow fever victim.

Masonry or iron fences surround many burial plots, and some graves are marked by a cross built into the brick wall encasing the plot.

The new section, "Flat Fields," opened in 1945 on land donated by the Cooper family. For a while, these graves were adorned with angel figurines, flowerpots, and flags, until the cemetery started looking cluttered and the extraneous materials were banned. Still, some decorations creep back. The living like to remember their dead at Bosque Bello; according to cemetery records, over 4,000 souls rest in peace there...excluding Luc Aury, of course, although he's probably buried somewhere in Bosque Bello, perhaps underneath a newer grave. It is unlikely, however, that his moaning spirit is at peace. Docent Sansbury reported that a girl riding her bike through the cemetery recently had the handlebars violently wrenched awry by an unseen force, causing her to fall.

If you believe in such things, it is easy to believe that in the dark beautiful woods of Bosque Bello, the depraved spirit of Luc Aury still has an appointment or two to keep with Fernandina citizens.

Visitor Information

Bosque Bello Cemetery
1320 North 14th Street
Fernandina Beach, FL 32034

Chapter 18

FLORIDA HOUSE INN

...before dying I want to share my verses of the soul.

—Jose Marti
"A Sincere Man Am I"

The Haunting

As told by Steve Sansbury, volunteer docent for the Amelia Island Museum of History:

This particular establishment advertises that it has spirits. If you'll look at the sign, it says, "Food, Lodging, and Spirits."

This is the oldest boarding establishment in the state of Florida. Many famous people stayed here: Ulysses S. Grant when he was president, movie stars Mary Pickford and Oliver Hardy, and Jose Marti, the man who started the Cuban revolution against Spain in the late nineteenth century.

The lyrics to the Cuban anthem "Guantanamera" were taken from a poem written by Marti. He was thrown out of Cuba, came to Florida to run guns to Cuba with a local man. Finally, he went back to Cuba and started up the revolution. He was a great writer, patriot, and poet, but not much of a military man; he was one of the first ones killed in the revolution.

Over the years, all kinds of things happen at the Florida Inn. Things move around. In the office, they'll put something down, come back, and it's gone. Then they find it somewhere else.

They've seen an apparition: a lady in a long black dress, standing between the two buildings watching them set up for breakfast when there was no one of that description staying at the hotel.

More recently, one morning they heard a terrible noise in the bathroom; they ran in and there was no one there, but the seat had been ripped off the toilet. Although, maybe it was just some lady, mad that her husband had left the toilet seat flipped up again.

This was a hotel for railroad workers. One of the railroad men lived here with his wife and baby, and guests often say that they hear a baby crying when there is no baby staying in the hotel.

Day and night at The Florida House Inn.

However, ghost hunters don't camp at the curb, and the name of the Florida House Inn is not high on the list of paranormal orb imagers. Although the upended toilet seat may have disconcerted a ghost unfamiliar with twenty-first century bathrooms, no one has ever sighted the more interesting apparitions of Marti, Grant, or Broward. Ms. De Vries in her book, *Ghosts of Amelia*, says that Annie Leddy's presence is detected by the odor of lavender, and that the hard-working businesswoman still oversees daily operations.

The History

Housing was usually available, in bordellos, for the pirates, the slave traders, and the other unsavory boulevardiers generated under Fernandina Beach's eight flags. Contracted laborers objected, but it wasn't until the late 1850s, when David Yulee, "the father of Florida railroads," built the antebellum Florida House Inn for his railroad workers. Trustees of the Florida Railroad

Company sold Yulee the lot for $300. According to a Department of the Interiors Historic Buildings Survey done in the 1970s, the architect was unknown, but it was a typical boarding house of the late nineteenth century, and considered one of the most "home-like" in Florida: a two-story frame house with a central hall, four rooms, a front porch, and no indoor plumbing. Although little of the original building remains according to Nassau County property records, (the oldest part of the Florida House is the building located at 23 South Third Street) the inn was built close to what was then the first passenger terminal of Yulee's railroad.

In 1873, the inn was sold for $2,600 to Thomas and Anne Leddy. Thomas Leddy, head of the military police during the Civil War, and a Provost Marshal of Northern Florida during Post-Civil War reconstruction, took out a mortgage on the inn with his wife, Anne, in 1873. He died shortly after, of gangrene, and Anne ran the Florida House from then on. It was a popular hotel and she made it a success, expanding the property and adding rooms. Leddy, or her heirs, owned it until 1940.

If its ghost story is discombobulated and random, it may help to consider the setting the inn provided for the prestigious history of its temporary inhabitants. Ulysses S. Grant didn't just stay at the Florida House Inn; he hosted a campaign reception in the dining room. Jose Marti, Cuban freedom fighter, didn't just bunk at the Florida House Inn. He plotted the overthrow of the Spanish government, using the inn as his base for running guns to Cuba on a tugboat called *The Three Friends*, owned and piloted by a man who would become the nineteenth governor of Florida: Napoleon Bonaparte Broward (Chapter 7).

Today, the Florida House Inn is a registered National Historic Place and offers sixteen rooms with quaint names such as "Railroad Twin" and "Grand Queen;" one of the suites is fitted out as a faux log cabin. The building also hosts The Mermaid Bar and a restaurant, The Southern Dining Room, that serves southern-style entrees, such as fried chicken, gumbo, and strawberry shortcake. The inn is within easy walking distance of the downtown Fernandina Beach historic district.

It is safe to say that whether or not spirits discombobulate on the grounds, the green building festooned with Fernandina's eight flags holds a lot of historic soul in the old towne.

Visitor Information

Florida House Inn & Mermaid Bar
20-23 South 3rd Street
Fernandina Beach, FL 32034
www.floridahouseinn.com

Chapter 19

Fort Clinch State Park

The problem here wasn't war—it was living.

—George Berninger
Fort Clinch Historian

The Haunting

Florida scholar Robert Thompson says that ghostly spirits "speak to the assurance we need of life after death."

Try telling that to the cashier at the visitor center/gift shop at Fort Clinch, who looks offended when tourists ask about stories of the spirits of Union soldiers, Confederate soldiers, General Duncan Lamont Clinch…anyone. As so often happens at state and national parks, she gives an exasperated look and the cold shoulder:

> *Ghosts? Not a bit of it. There were no battles, here, no cemeteries. No reason for ghosts.*

Lee Bledsoe, a Civil War reenactor in a Union uniform, is a man who is reputed to be so knowledgeable about Fort Clinch that "he knows all of the bricks by first name." He had this to say:

> *I've been here nineteen years, and I've never seen a ghost. I have a partner here thirty-five years. He never saw anything. This place was never in combat, people who got sick were transported. There is not one recorded death.*

However certain Lee may be of his facts, history states that the location of Fort Clinch, a seacoast fortification, was a military region as far back as 1736. Furthermore, in the 1830s, the Seminole Indian Wars were raging under the command of General Clinch himself. It is possible that the fort was built over the remains of some Indians' and soldiers' graves.

Atlantic Ocean lapping on the distinctive curved shoreline located on the northern tip of Amelia Island.

There is more evidence of soldier mortality at Fort Clinch. According to an article by Benjamin Price, published in the *Fernandina Beach New Leader* in 2006, during the Civil War era, twenty soldiers died within seven months at Fort Clinch. They died primarily of disease, dysentery, and malnutrition. Reporter Price captions a picture of the fort's hospital ward as, "the last sight for hundreds of men who died of disease and infection." Two Union soldiers, Daniel Morgan and James Oliver, were interred somewhere in Fernandina Beach's Bosque Bello Cemetery (Chapter 17). In 2006, official federal markers for the two Fort Clinch soldiers were erected under a cypress tree near the graves of veterans of the Spanish-American War. The article further states that the old cemetery was also the site for the unmarked graves of three other Fort Clinch soldiers who were "shot for desertion."

A Fort Clinch ghost story, published October 31, 1997 in the *Florida Times-Union,* was based on a story by former Fort Clinch Ranger George Berninger:

> *One full moon in July, two volunteers saw four ghosts in Civil War garb come out of a tunnel and then over a wall. The next year, the volunteers made sure they were there again during the July full moon. Sure enough, three ghosts came down the northwest bastion tunnel, across the parade ground, and started up the ramp.*
>
> *The volunteers called to them, "Where's the fourth man?"*
>
> *"He's sick tonight. Couldn't come," one of the figures called back.*

The History

The Fort Clinch address is a meandering three miles on a sun- and shadow-dappled road bordered by oak, ash, and elm trees draped with Spanish moss. Trees meet over tourist's heads, branches intertwining. A cadre of cyclists passes on one side and huge sand dunes mount on the other.

There is a visitor center, gift shop, and bookstore at the entrance to Fort Clinch, and the Amelia River Camp in the other direction. Everything else about the Fort Clinch experience pertains to the Civil War, although no battles were fought here and the fort was never attacked.

Walking out of the visitor center is a sign shaped like a Union soldier, reading:

> *1864—You are about to enter a US sea-coast fortification. The unit stationed here is the 1st New York Volunteer Engineers. If you see a soldier going about his duties don't be afraid to ask questions. He will tell you what he is doing and other details that will bring the history of Fort Clinch to life.*

When the brick walls and cannons of the fortress loom behind the elevated grounds on both sides of the dirt path, people tend to forget that they are basically sunburned Florida tourists in cargo pants and Disney T-shirts. Past

Garrison life at Fort Clinch in Fernandina Beach.

the grassy moat and down a brick tunnel, everyone emerges in a pentagonal parade field, where there are Union re-enactors everywhere, dressed as soldiers, miraculously sweat-free in their dark wool uniforms.

The fort was built by the United States government in 1847 and soldiers worked on it until 1861. Like most Florida forts, it is unfinished and, like most Florida forts, there is a good reason.

The fort was built of brick, and the US government was fussy about subsidizing southern sympathizers for masonry. Their expedient solution, after they'd already started and apparently taken enough guff from the locals, was to buy the bricks up north and import them to Amelia Island. Visitors can tell the difference between the northern and the southern bricks, integrated into the masonry walls, by their shades of color.

The US government abandoned the fort in 1861 around the same time that Florida announced it was seceding from the Union. So, the Southern Florida Militia held Fort Clinch until the Union army retook it in 1862. However, the main job for the US soldiers at the fort was construction, not military maneuvers. This was true throughout the Civil War, the Reconstruction period, and the Spanish-American War. Unlike the Spanish and British reenactors at the Castillo de San Marcos in St. Augustine with their loading of muskets, fancy regalia, and cannon fire, Fort Clinch reenactors are stuck

Visitors can tell the difference between the northern and the southern bricks, integrated into the masonry walls, by their shades of color.

with drab uniforms, and the boring regimen of garrison life, including laundry, infirmary, and livery duties.

So maybe it wasn't too amazing in 1924 when the US government put the fort on the market as real estate. As waterfront property, it was special. There was the sound of the Atlantic Ocean lapping on the distinctive curved shoreline located on the northern tip of Amelia Island. The fort overlooked the Cumberland sound, and provided gateways to the St. Mary and the Amelia rivers as well as the deep-water harbor of Fernandina Beach. A private party actually bought it in 1926, and promptly tried to flip the waterfront property by tearing down the fort. Fortunately, the mortar was too strong and all those years of government caretaking really paid off. We're talking about four and a half million bricks, with walls four and a half feet thick and twenty-six feet high, a tabby cannon ledge, and five masonry towers.

By 1935, the private owner was begging the government to take the fort back, which it did, probably at a discount. During the Great Depression, the Civilian Conservation Corps restored it, and the fort served as a Coast Guard station during World War II. It's been a state park ever since.

Fort Clinch, and the surrounding area, is available for camping, beaches, swimming in the Atlantic Ocean, hiking, bird trails, picnicking, bicycle trails and fishing. In addition, the fort offers candlelit nightly tours on some weekends and union garrison reenactments one weekend a month. What isn't reenacted is the sort of grim deprivation from which the Union soldiers suffered. This is something the war-hardened namesake of the fort knew a lot about.

There was a real-life General Clinch, and he resigned from the military in 1836, against the wishes of Andrew Jackson, and led a private life from there on. He died in Georgia a year or two before the government broke ground on the Florida fort that bears his name.

A North Carolinian by birth, he was dead long before the Civil War, but it is a great irony that the union garrison bears the name of a general who almost certainly would have fought for the rebel side in the Civil War. In fact, his son was a Confederate colonel who fought in the Battle of Olustee (Chapter 29).

Maybe General Clinch is the fourth man in the ghost story "who couldn't come" to the War Between the States.

Visitor Information

Fort Clinch State Park
2601 Atlantic Avenue
Fernandina Beach, FL32035
www.floridastateparks.org/fortclinch

Chapter 20

FRANKLINTOWN CEMETERY

Step softly, a dream lies buried here.
—John James Chenevert

The Haunting

Alice P. Youngblood recounted a conversation with longtime resident Morris Drummond during her visit to Franklintown in 1937 as transcribed in her "African American History" of Fernandina Beach. Drummond, a son of slaves, told her what he termed a "true" ghost story about a voice he and his sister Rebecca kept hearing when they were three and four years old. The first time the children heard it they were playing in the yard. Drummond said that the voice called "low and soft, come from far, den it would come near." He said it sounded like his mother's voice. The voice would beckon them deep into the woods. They continued to follow the voice even when it got dark. A search by the other slaves recovered the children. There was speculation that they were running away.

The children were left to fend for themselves during the day because their mother was a slave on the Harrison Plantation, and she spent her days picking and tending sea cotton instead of her children. But she was clearly distressed by the children's wanderings and by their story. Drummond said his mother whipped them.

But that wasn't the end of the voice. Sometimes, a day or two would pass before the children heard it again, but it always returned, beckoning them, sometimes moaning, always calling, and always, always the children followed it. He said that he and Rebecca suffered a lot of "whippings about dat voice."

Finally, his mother reached the end of her rope. She told Drummond, "Don't you tell me no voice a calling you today, I gwine bust you open if you tell me a voice callin' you."

Drummond said his uncle, an elderly man, sitting near the fire "roasting two pomegranates" for the children, overheard the conversation. He told their

A view of the Franklintown Cemetery bordered by homes with swimming pools.

mother, "Now look ahear, don't talk dat way to dem children. Let me hear what dey got to say."

When he heard the children's story, their uncle said:

> *"Now see here Ma, dey is right. Dey is been hearing a voice, dats de evil one, dats de evil voice. Now let me tell you how to get rid of dat old evil spirit. Just don't pay no attention to him. Dat make him mad and he go away. Nex time he call, jest stan dar and laugh and say, 'We know you, we ain't a coming."*

Drummond and his sister began to hear the voice less often. He speculated that the evil spirit behind the voice was trying to "fool him" thinking he'd forget. When the voice called, he and Rebecca would start to follow, but then they'd remember their uncle's advice and stay. They'd laugh at the voice. And it would stop calling them.

A month later, the voice called again. The children stayed put and laughed. The voice persisted, "a moaning and a crying and a calling." The children didn't follow. One day, Drummond said, "Dere a loud noise lak somebody's a running through the brush." He said they never heard the voice again.

He was wrong about that. The voice came back almost fifty years later. It came back with a vengeance.

The History

It is very easy to miss the sign, more for the incongruousness of its location than for its size. Anyone can drive up and down A1A for years without spotting it. You can stop at the gas station or fire station for directions to no avail. No one seems to know where it is. But it's there—a blur, visible from the corner of an eye. Pull onto the shoulder of A1A, a leafy enclave. There it is, in script letters: Franklintown Cemetery. It is a freestanding sign posted near a fence surrounding a gated community: Plantation Pointe.

In order to see the cemetery, visitors have to call the phone number on the sign and set up an appointment for a tour. The irony of a cemetery for slaves and for their descendents, enclosed within the grounds of a gated community named Plantation, is not lost on anyone, except perhaps developers. It is not lost on caretaker George Green, either. He is a retired army combat engineer with three tours of duty, including Vietnam, yet he remains first and foremost a former Franklintown resident. He is a direct descendant of slaves, all of whom are buried beneath the leafy soft ground that punctuates wealthy homeowner's backyards and swimming pools. His voice is the one that you hear when you call the number on the Franklintown sign.

> *"They tried to force us out," Green says of the white developers. "We had a tug of war. They tried to block us from coming in—put a chain on the fence. We came out here and cut it out."*

The history of Franklintown goes back to the Harrison Plantation; generational slave owners burned their plantation down in 1862 rather than let Union forces get their hands on it. The Union soldiers released the Harrison slaves, about twelve families, who settled on 200 acres just north of the old plantation. The Harrisons deeded two acres of land to their former slaves to bury their dead. The name "Franklintown" came from a freed slave, Franklin E. Town, who tried to purchase some of the land in 1872; he didn't succeed, but the name stuck.

Flanked by the Atlantic Ocean and the Amelia River, Franklintown settlers worked hard and lived off the land and the sea for 100 years. "It was nice," Green was quoted saying in a 1998 article in *Folio Weekly*. "We had a road right to the beach. We had all kinds of sweet plums, persimmons, grapes. My granddaddy had a boat ramp on the riverside. We'd go out there oystering and crabbing, we'd go out in the woods and hunt."

In 1949, the state of Florida built a road right through Franklintown. In the 1980s, it was not unusual for counties to plow highways directly through the centers of generational black neighborhoods. Zora Neale Hurston's stomping ground in Eatonville was subjected to the same territorial invasion, but Eatonville fought back and won. Franklintown, for whatever reasons, did not.

Free standing sign to the cemetery outside the gates of Plantation Pointe housing development.

Union Carbide bought up some of the acreage for strip mining. Residents moved half a mile up the road and formed "New Franklintown."

"They moved us up to where the tennis courts are now," says Green. "That's where our church was."

Alice P. Youngblood noted in her 1937 Nassau county Federal Writer's Project that Morris Drummond and his wife were examples of "old time Negroes" and "humble to a marked degree." She saw that as a good thing and, in 1937, it was probably a common quality. Nevertheless, it cost Franklintown residents the literal roof over their heads. New Franklintown was another casualty in the same old story: a black community booted off their land once a wealthy developer got wind of the scent of profits.

Since Union Carbide never obtained permits to strip mine the land, they sold it, in 1970, to the future developers of the Amelia Island Plantation for 4.65 million dollars. At the time, it was the largest land purchase ever made in Nassau County and comprised the entire south end of Amelia Island. Developers secured the rest of the land from New Franklintown residents for a pittance. Former Franklintown resident Willie Stewart was quoted in a 1998 article for *Folio Weekly*: "We each got a thousand dollars a piece."

The Franklintown residents, one house, and the United Methodist Franklintown Church were moved to American Beach (Chapter 24). George Green was off fighting the Vietnam war. When he returned, his home was gone.

But the Franklintown Cemetery would not and could not be moved; it is against Florida Statute 872, Florida's Unmarked Burial Law, and a third degree felony, "to willfully and knowingly disturb an unmarked burial or burials." Violators face substantial prison time and fines.

A developer, unaware of such fine points, turned his attention to the two-acre cemetery where former Harrison Plantation slaves lay in eternal rest.

> *"He called this the bone yard," Green said of the developer. "He said he had 40 new houses to build. He just wanted us out. We had to get the newspaper out here about his trespassing. If he'd had his way, there wouldn't a been a cemetery."*

Although the Harrisons deeded the cemetery to Franklintown residents, Green claims the paperwork mysteriously disappeared from official records. This left residents with no clear title to the land, only "perpetual use;" Franklintown did not own the land, only the burial rights.

Finally, a man named Duval bought the land, and the Franklintown Cemetery Association, and Morris Drummond in particular, worked with him for a year. Duval ended up deeding Franklintown descendants one half acre of their original two acres of cemetery. Houses priced between $300,000 and a million dollars were dug over the acreage of the former cemetery. What happened to any unearthed human remains is anyone's guess. But nothing was ever reported.

The facts rankle Green, a soft-spoken man with a steely tenacity to this historic scrap of land preserved amidst the spacious stone facades and the spurious cobblestone driveways of a luxurious gated community. But there is no friction between the residents and the caretakers. A middle-aged woman with gray hair leans out of her screened porch to wave at Green.

"How ya doing?" she asks. They chat for a few minutes from opposite sides of the fence. If the residents of Plantation Pointe are upset about the cemetery, they certainly aren't showing it. If anything, they seem to welcome the company.

Green says, "The people around here let us know if anyone messes around."

The cemetery is covered with leaves and the ground is soft. From the bowers of hickory trees, squirrels screech over the traffic racket of A1A. The trees are big with visible roots intersecting the soil like veins. Green says there

Grave of Lena Hopkins, a nineteenth century descendant of the Harrison Plantation slaves.

are between 100 to 200 graves within the confines of the half-acre cemetery, and graves for descendants of Franklintown slaves are still dug here. So many markers have been displaced or eroded, when a funeral approaches, Green pokes the soft ground with a stick, to see if it hits anything solid, in order to scope out a new gravesite.

> "When I started keeping the rows, it was growed up bad. You couldn't see nothing. Someone come in here with a Bush Hog and knocked down the wooden markers. But everybody got a section. There's the Drummonds. There's the Means. There's the Hopkins. I'm a Hopkins."

Silk flowers grace several graves. Green's great- grandfather, Gabriel Means, a Union soldier in the Civil War, lies beneath a military marker. From the Drummond clan, there is Morris and his wife, and two little girls who died of yellow fever buried side by side. There is a Harrison here, too, an interracial relative of the slave owners. Green brushes dirt off a crudely formed block of cement with printed letters that look as though they were drawn with a stick. "This is Nellie Mae Jones, my granddaddy's niece. She died in 1999."

Under the shade of a tall tree, amid the pinecones, the leaves, the hickory nuts, one may listen for the voice that Morris Drummond and his sister Rebecca heard so clearly, a voice so beguiling that it lured them away from play and diminished all fear of their mother's wrath. But today there is nothing except the sounds of traffic and the squirrels. It's clear that it was the millionaires and the big business interests that lured Franklintown residents away long ago. Still, it all started with an unknown voice in the wilderness. The residents of Franklintown followed that voice, and gave in to temptation. Now all that's left are the dead and the mute testimony of their half acre of land.

Visitor Information

Franklintown Cemetery
off A1A at Plantation Point Drive
Fernandina Beach, FL 32035

Chapter 21

NaNa at American Beach

I, too, sing America.

—**Langston Hughes**
"I, Too"

The Haunting

This is more of a potential ghost story, than a ghost story in itself. It involves a former heiress and opera singer turned environmentalist, an historic beach site, and a sixty-foot sand dune named NaNa.

The entrance to American Beach is a little way across the street from the old Franklintown Cemetery (Chapter 20), on Ocean Boulevard, on the Atlantic side. You can drive on the beach, and risk the soft sand, or scout the small side streets. Not much goes on. Tourists may see two guys conferring over the open hood of an old car, but not much else. No one is on the beach, as a rule, except the sea gulls, lots of them, undisturbed and congregated on the white sand near the surge of salt water. Tourists may see some old boarded-up buildings on American Beach and the resorts and the condos in the distance.

They may see NaNa.

It stops people short. NaNa is a white mountain of sand, the biggest most people will ever see. It makes every other sand dune in Florida look like a pitiful mound, or like the proverbial molehill. NaNa is, in fact, the biggest sand dune system in Florida.

The fact that it is there at all is nothing short of a miracle. Just north and south of American Beach are the wealthy neighboring communities: Amelia Island Plantation and the Ritz Carlton Resort—huge commercial ventures whose pervasive sprawl could easily tamp even the monstrous mound that is NaNa down to a tennis court or a putting green. Yet it hasn't happened.

There is a reason for that.

According to the roadside marker, which local residents coughed up $2,000 to erect, there once was a "Beach Lady," a dreadlocked African-American woman named MaVynee Betsch. She was American Beach royalty; the great-granddaughter of the man who founded the place, a voice teacher, and an opera singer who lived abroad. Yet, she came home, at some point, and she spent the last twenty-five years of her life, and all of her fortune, preserving American Beach, and NaNa, in particular, from the kind of encroaching developmental interests that took over... well...Amelia Island in the 1970s. Appearing on CNN and other national news outlets, she succeeded in saving nine acres of American Beach, including NaNa. The National Park Service maintains it as an historical site.

So where is the ghost? No one sees footprints in the sand, or hears voices in the wind. Yet Marcus Franklin's 2004 *St. Petersburg Times* article "History in the sand" predicts the potential evolution of a new haunted site. After living in a tiny mobile home on American Beach for over two decades, the Beach Lady died of cancer in 2005. She wanted to be cremated, and she wanted her ashes spread on NaNa. Then she vowed to deal with those most likely to disturb her life's work and her last remains. She said:

> *I have no qualms about the future of American Beach. I'm going to haunt these white developers even when I'm gone.*

So far, her threat is working.

The History

Amelia Island, like most of Florida, was a rampant hotbed of racism and segregation in the Post-Civil War South. Until 1884, black people weren't "allowed" on most of Florida's northeast beaches except for Butler's Beach near St. Augustine, a pavilion in Franklintown in Fernandina Beach, and the southern end of Jacksonville Beach.

Florida's first black millionaire, an insurance magnate named Abraham Lincoln (A. L.) Lewis (Betsch's great-grandfather), bought thirty-three acres of American Beach in 1935, solely to provide beachfront property for Amelia Island's African-American community, in particular his employees at the Afro-American Life Insurance Company. Eventually, Lewis's beachfront acquisition expanded to 200 acres. The location became the place to be for the African-American community seeking respite from Jim Crow laws. An American Beach nightclub, Evan's Rendezvous, hosted singing legends such as Cab Calloway, Ray Charles, Louis Armstrong, Billie Daniels. Zora Neale Hurston hung out at juke joints, took notes for her books and for the Works Progress Administration. By 1960, it was common for the beach to accommodate a crowd of 2,000 in one day.

Revetment project for American Beach donated by the Afro-American Pension Bureau.

NaNa at American Beach.

It was Hurricane Dora and the Civil Rights Act that ended American Beach's heyday. Both occurred in the mid-'60s and scattered the beach-loving tourists; one, because of sand erosion, and damage to buildings and resorts, the other because of desegregation. African-Americans didn't have to drive to Amelia Island for fun in the sun; they could go anywhere. Many chose beaches closer to their homes.

Today, its residents include some new beachfront property buyers and most of the descendants of Franklintown. The Franklintown United Methodist Church, on Lewis Street, is still a gathering place for community events, as well as a house of worship. And there are prestigious antecedents connected to American Beach. According to the spring newsletter for The American Beach Property Association, President Obama "recently nominated Circuit Judge Brian Davis of American Beach to a US District Judgeship in Florida's Middle District."

Still, American Beach is, overall, an isolated stretch of sand. Evan's Rendezvous is closed, and aside from some private rentals, there is only one hotel on Greeg Street: The American Beach Villas. Developers have taken over all but 120 acres. Rumor has it, they'd like to take more. This brings the reader back to the historically preserved NaNa.

NaNa is no great shakes compared to a dune in Fallon, Nevada, which boasts a pillar of sand almost 400 feet high. NaNa doesn't "boom," "squeak," "roar," or exhibit any acoustical talents (unlike The Beach Lady) as many dunes do because of sand compression. Nevertheless, it is an attractive snow-white dune, towering over American Beach, veined with beach grass and admirably performing its task of buffer between State Road A1A and the Atlantic Ocean.

There have been no tales of Beach Lady apparitions or arias from the underworld rustling the sea oats. People miss her, though, and bloggers text wistfully about the void the vibrant woman's absence has left and about the lonely granular monument to her efforts. They write that the Beach Lady is still walking the dunes...

Yet, Betsch made herself clear. As long as NaNa endures, everything is cool. If plans are prepared to make the dune disappear, developers need to watch out...for a dreadlocked ghost.

Visitor Information

NaNa on American Beach
www.historicamericanbeach.com

Location: On the southern end of the Atlantic Ocean side, north of the Amelia Island Plantation; off A1A, access on Ocean Boulevard between Burney Road and Lewis Street.

Chapter 22

NETTIE THOMPSON HOUSE

I did not wish to live what was not life...

—**Henry David Thoreau**
Walden

The Haunting

From Penny Sansbury, volunteer docent at the Amelia Island Museum of History on the Amelia Island Ghost Tour:

Pratt Thompson had this house built for his wife, Nettie, and she was definitely afraid of fires. So she insisted her house be built of brick. It was the first brick home in the historic district. There were other brick buildings, but they were commercial buildings. You know the history of old towns like this: there's always a fire that takes out all the houses because they're close together, because they're wooden, and they just burn. She was insistent that her house be brick.

The tragic thing is that she did die in a fire. She died in a fire in a Miami hotel. A wooden hotel. But one theory of ghosts is that they go back to where they were happiest. Nettie is a ghost here. There are stories that go back at least sixty years of Nettie Thompson haunting this house. There are all sorts of tales of people seeing her image coming down the center stairs, carrying a candle. They hear her taffeta petticoats rustling, they smell the beeswax, they could have all those sensory images, and she comes down the stairs and takes a left and walks through the wall. Well, in the old days, that would've been where the summer kitchen was.

She tends to move things. People say she's very friendly, not malevolent at all, but they do a "Nettie test" by putting something on a table at night. It's moved to another table the next morning. If you drop something on the floor, she'll pick it up.

Someone took a picture of the house forty years ago, and a woman showed up in the second story window: a woman in a black taffeta dress. Sometimes, from the street, you can see the curtain rustling, but the owner says there's no fan, there's no heat. Sometimes that curtain is really moving a lot.

Everybody says that when you live here, you can just expect Nettie to be one of your roommates. The owners had a dog, a miniature poodle who would bark at the door, but there was no one there. Their cat just ran away; he wouldn't stay. But the owners say they're not afraid. Nettie is a benign presence.

The History

Designed by architect John H. Edges, the house is actually one of three Thompson homes in a row, built next to each other for the immediate family. William N. Thompson, a Florida senator and a former Confederate soldier, purchased them in 1873. (The roots of the confederacy ran deep in the Thompson men; their uncle, Scott McGehee, wrote the articles of cessation when Florida seceded from the Union in 1861.)

One of the houses, built for Thompson's sister, was called "the Lucy cottage." The brick house went to his brother, Pratt, and his sister-in-law, Nettie. She, of course, is notorious for never leaving.

And who can blame her? It's a gorgeous house with octagonal bay windows. In addition to its brick foundation, it has a brick chimney, sidelights, a skylight around the entrance, which has two porticos, and a two-story gabled porch. There are a few peculiarities, such as the keyhole shields, which were used to keep people from peeking through. On the other hand, since Senator William Thompson lived next door to his brother and his sister, a little privacy was the most natural thing in the world.

Today, the Thompson House is part of the historic district of Fernandina Beach. Since the house is not listed in the National Historic register, in the past it has been marketed as office space. Today, it's a private residence owned by Brian and Melanie Grimley. They use the address to run a very small restaurant, less than 700 square feet, called Lulu's Place at the Thompson House. Brian is from England, an amateur chef, who used to run a full-service restaurant in Virginia where he, like William Thompson, lived for many years. The menu features seafood with a New Orleans flair.

There is not much hope of catching a glimpse of Nettie since she confines herself to the stairwell, chairs, and second story. Perhaps you can see the curtains rustling or catch a glimpse of her from the window. It seems she's never quite reconciled herself to death, and prefers whatever semblance of life the Thompson House still offers.

Visitor Information

Nettie Thompson House
11 South 7th Street
Fernandina Beach, FL 32034
www.lulusamelia.com

Nettie Thompson's nineteenth century brick house.

NETTIE THOMPSON HOUSE

Chapter 23

THE PALACE SALOON

How does a pirate know he exists? He thinks, therefore he arghhs.

—Bob Randall

The Haunting

From Steve Sansbury –a volunteer docent conducting the Ghost Tour for the Amelia Island Museum of History:

Louis G. Hirth always had his eye on this building. He wanted a fancy upscale saloon here in Fernandina in 1904. Everybody in the world came here because it was the nicest saloon and because of the people—like the Carnegies—who would tie up their ships, unpack their freight, and meet in the Palace Saloon.

Edison was here, Cecil B. DeMille, the Duponts. Budweiser Augie Busch helped design the bar. On either side of the bar, there are wooden carvings of women, with their arms extended upward, holding up the top of the bar. They're called caryatids: a female form, really popular in Greek architecture. One of the buildings in the Acropolis is called the Fortune Caryatids.

Now these Palace Saloon caryatids have real low décolletage. And everyone knows when people get into a bar they want to drink and gamble. A man named Charles Beresford, Uncle Charlie, the bartender here for over fifty years, invented a game. Here's how he played: If you flipped a quarter, and it stuck in the caryatid's décolletage, you got a free drink—a billion to one shot. At the end of the night, Charlie swept the quarters up off the floor. Free money. This game went on for a while.

Uncle Charlie died in the '60s...well, that was a tragic thing here on the island. They had a big wake. The next day they opened up the bar, and that night they played the game. A young man went to sweep up the quarters...and an icy hand stopped him.

No one ever played that game again.

Exterior of The Palace Saloon dominating the corner of Centre Street.

The famous caryatids, holding up the ceiling of the bar.

The History

The saloon was built as a haberdashery in 1878, but by the end of the century, German immigrant Louis Hirth wanted the "brick block" anchored in a deep foundation of oyster shells and dominating the corner of Centre and 2nd Streets in downtown Fernandina Beach.

Fernandina Beach was a fashionable harbor town, lined with sailing vessels, and with a couple of dozen bars and brothels. Hirth wanted something better—a "ship captain's saloon"—and he got it when he saved up the money to buy the building in 1901.

Five years later, he hired bartender Charles Beresford, whose moniker, curiously, was the same as a popular Lord and Member of Parliament in England, affectionately known as Charlie B. Fernandina Beach's Beresford became known as Uncle Charlie, a man so inexplicably intertwined with his work that he slept in a room above the bar for fifty-four years.

View of the upstairs apartment of former bartender "Uncle Charlie" Beresford who tended The Palace Saloon for half a century.

Hirth was not so humble. He was a guy who wore diamond stickpins, diamond rings, and a diamond-encrusted watch fob, and he spared no expense on his dream of a high-class saloon.

He lined the ceiling with embossed tin and installed imported marble and granite for wall borders. It was a standup bar, made of hand-carved mahogany, including columns and a brass rail. There were brass cuspidors and a gas-fired lighter that his customers and friends, the Carnegies, used to set fire to paper money to light their expensive cigars.

Most piquant, however, were the wall murals painted in 1903 by Roy Kennard. Kennard lived up north and was visiting family in Fernandina Beach when he ran into Hirth on Centre Street one day. Hirth offered Kennard $300 to paint the murals, although, later, Kennard admitted he would have done it for nothing. He thought Shakespeare would be a good theme for his work, so he copied Portia and Shylock from the cover of a theater advertising *The Merchant of Venice*. He painted a mural of *Pickwick* and *The Quibbling Barristers*. So beloved were the murals that when a fire swept through the bar in February of 1999, local editorials bemoaned, most of all, not the absence of a sprinkler system, but the loss of the bar's ambience embodied in the murals. To everyone's relief, the bar was restored and the murals, according to a Palace bartender, touched up by a relative of Kennard.

The Palace Saloon is actually three bars in one: there is the main bar, guarded by a life-sized pirate statue; Uncle Charlie's Sports Bar; and the nightclub, Sheffields. Christmas Day and New Year's are big days at the bar, and an annually sponsored 5K road race takes place every April.

Today, a solid presence along the fifty blocks of the historic district, the saloon enjoys the reputation as the oldest continuously operated saloon in the nation—it was an ice-cream parlor during Prohibition (*wink, wink*)—and a popular gathering place for locals, tourists, and pirate aficionados. Tourists who have visited Fernandina Beach several times, have never found so much as a place to sit in the bar or at adjoining tables, which are often occupied by pirates and their "wenches" in full costume, including eye patches.

The sea captains and the freewheeling Carnegies are gone, but Uncle Charlie, generations of faithful revelers, and Hirth's dream, remain.

Visitor Information

The Palace Saloon
117 Centre Street
Fernandina Beach, FL 32034-4236
www.thepalacesaloon.com

Chapter 24

Phelan-Verot House

Believers, look up—take courage. The angels are nearer than you think.

—**Billy Graham**

The Haunting

Told by Steven Sansbury, volunteer docent for the Amelia Island Museum of History:

The women who lived in the Phelan-Verot House, after the Civil War, were called the Sisters of LePuy, because they came from LePuy, France, or the Holy Sisters, or, later, the Angels of Mercy. They came here to teach the children of former slaves how to read and write and they taught the children in the Catholic Church.

Father Verot, the Catholic bishop, came to visit, and what he found was that the nuns were teaching the children during the day, and at night, they were sleeping on the floor of the church. The Bishop said, "We can't have that, it's wrong." So he bought the Phelan-Verot House for the nuns.

Now in 1877, like in a lot of southern ports—Norfolk, Savannah, Charleston, New Orleans—yellow fever hit Fernandina Beach. The nuns took care of the sick here in this house. The people who lived in the community were so scared of the yellow fever in the house that they would not approach it; they'd throw bags of food on the porch rather than risk contamination. They'd throw bolts of cloth through the window. The cloth was for the nuns to sew shrouds for the dead.

The townspeople did not know that mosquitoes caused yellow fever. They fired cannons into the air on Centre Street to kill the yellow fever microbes. They also burned big tubs of asphalt and pitch.

The nuns, tending to people who were unconscious, put the legs of the beds in basins of water to keep the bugs from crawling up the bed rails. Of course, the mosquitoes were breeding in the water, biting the sick people and spreading yellow fever. Two of the nuns caught yellow fever and died. When Father Verot came back, he found out that the nuns were buried in the backyard. If you're Catholic, you have to be buried on consecrated ground. So he found two plots in Bosque Bello Cemetery, consecrated the ground, and prepared to have the nuns moved.

The nuns were ordained in the order of St. Joseph, and in St. Augustine, they have a museum in the chapel. In the museum are two diaries side by side. The diaries detail the

The Phelan-Verot House where the holy sisters of LePuy nursed yellow fever victims in 1877.

accounts of two workmen who exhumed the bodies of the nuns. They had to check to make sure they had the right bodies. When they opened the caskets, they expected the smell of decay, of rot. Instead, they smelled roses. The bodies of the nuns were perfectly intact, rosy and soft, looking as though they had just gone to sleep. There was no decay whatsoever.

In the Catholic Church, that is known as incorruptible, a sign of people who are eligible for sainthood. The nuns were reinterred back in Bosque Bello Cemetery.

The Phelan-Verot house is privately owned today, and the woman who lives here has seen the nuns. She sees them on the staircase, she sees them rocking. We know from the records that one of the nuns who died was only 4'11". The apparition the owner claims to see, she describes as "a very short nun."

Every year, the owner's Christmas decorations are thrown out into the yard. Someone doesn't like them. One of the volunteers from the museum was here at a party one night, and one of the pictures just flew off the wall. The owner walked over and put it back. "It's just the nuns," she said. "They do that all the time."

If you gotta have a ghost, a nun is the kind to have. We want to rename this story and call it, "Nuns and Roses."

The History

It sounds unlikely that any of the saintly nuns, known as the "Angels of Mercy" during the 1877 yellow fever epidemic in Fernandina Beach, would return as apparitions who fling Christmas decorations on the lawn in a fit of phantom pique. To start at the beginning, it may help to know that the first name of the house derived from another couple entirely: William and Sarah Phelan owned the house on 4th Street for twenty-one years.

David Yulee hired William Phelan to help lay the railroad tracks for The Florida Railroad Company in 1856, which may explain why Phelan bought the house when it was built in 1866. In 1876, Sarah Phelan sold it for $900 to Bishop Augustine Verot, who wanted a house to shelter the nuns he recruited from his hometown in LePuy, France. The nuns' job was to educate and to confirm the white and black children of Fernandina Beach.

According to local Fernandina Beach historian and author Suzanne Hardee, Bishop Verot was "an avowed Confederate" but after the Civil War, he saw the need to educate the freed slaves. In eight months, he taught the French nuns to speak and to write English and then he sent them off to Fernandina Beach.

These nuns had a hard time of it even before the yellow fever epidemic hit. Living on alms, the nuns in their black habits were vilified by the local townspeople, who called them "devils, doing the devil's work."

Then, in August of 1877, yellow fever entered Fernandina through a West Indies ship whose sailors, infected with the virus, were not quarantined and walked freely about the town. A local family of four, whose menfolk had been working on the doomed ship, was the first to perish.

Yellow Fever was regarded in the same way that Europeans regarded the black plague. The disease could die out quickly, but more often, it swept through entire towns, affecting almost every family. The situation in Fernandina Beach was even more acute, because all of the doctors succumbed to the disease and died in the early weeks of the epidemic (Chapter 26).

In this environment, the nuns quickly became heroines, opening their home to the afflicted, nursing them night and day, and sewing shrouds for the unfortunate victims who died. It is true that the townspeople were too terrified of yellow fever to approach the house, but they did try to help by throwing food, bolts of cloth, even rocks wrapped with needles and thread on the porch of "the nun's house" from a distance.

Mother Celenie and twenty-six-year-old Sister de Sales died in September within eight hours of each other. Buried in Bosque Bello Cemetery under two simple crosses, their markers bear only their names and the dates of their births and deaths. In all, according to an article by William Straight in the 1971 *Journal of the Florida Medical Association*, the Fernandina Beach population in 1877 was 3,000 people. Over 1,400 people fell ill, and ninety-five people died of yellow fever.

The yellow fever epidemic ended in the fall, but the nuns stayed on in the Phelan-Verot house until 1882, when they left to reside in their own convent and to open a school. St. Joseph's Academy, named for the order of the nuns, endured until 1961, when it was sold to St. Michael's parish. There is still a plaque with the name "Sisters of St. Joseph" on an exterior wall of the St. Michael's School.

In the ensuing years, the Phelan-Verot house fell into disrepair, and by the late twentieth century, it faced city condemnation hearings. The years had taken their toll, and the house was in bad shape. It suffered from wood rot and termites.

Trees were growing through the porch.

Briefly owned in 1990 by George Sheffield (owner of the Bailey House and the Palace Saloon), he flipped the house for a profit to the local First Baptist Church, which was more interested in the lot than in the decrepit historic house. The church wanted the house moved (which in its poor condition would have irrevocably destroyed it) or removed in order to use the grounds as a sorely needed parking lot for its congregation.

The Amelia Island Fernandina Restoration Foundation (AIFRF) was outraged by the Baptist Church's plan, and thus began a series of letters, newspaper editorials, and a public outcry to save the Phelan-Verot house from extinction. Eventually, the AIFRF acquired the property and saved it from being torn down or carted off. Then the house sat for almost another decade until two handymen bought it and spent $40,000 to restore it, doing most of the work themselves.

The present owner, Pam Brown, lived in the restored nun's house for a year as a caretaker. In a 2000 article in *Amelia Islander Magazine*, Brown is quoted as saying "Perhaps the spirits of the deceased sisters still live here. When I was little and wouldn't behave, my mother would threaten to send me to a nunnery. Now I own one."

The house is small, just 1,600 square feet, a one-and-a-half-story wooden frame in the style called "Folk Victorian." There is a gable roof, dormer windows, and a transom over the front door. The original floors are still intact and the walls of the small interior rooms are papered in a custom Victorian design.

It is open to the public on the Amelia Island Museum of History's walking tour.

Is there a chance of sighting one or more of nuns during the tour? Given the compelling evidence of their beatitude, whether the spirits of Mother Celenie and Sister de Sales still walk the Phelan-Verot house is open to debate. If anyone has earned the right to ascend to heaven, it is these good women.

So many people have lived and died in the Phelan-Verot house that it is hard to say just who flings the Christmas decorations on the lawn. Perhaps the spirits of the sisters just want to clear the way for the missives of food, cloth, and stones wrapped with needles and thread that they relied on to take care of their yellow fever invalids.

Given their record of saintly service, perhaps they consider the Phelan-Verot house their own little patch of heaven on earth.

Visitor Information

Phelan-Verot House
116 N. 4th Street
Fernandina Beach, FL 32034

Chapter 25

Sliders Seaside Grill

If you're lucky enough to be at the beach, you're lucky enough.

—From a sign inside Sliders Seaside Grill
Anonymous

The Haunting

Who would have guessed that a murder occurring over a century ago on the lonely sand dunes of Fernandina Beach could, in some small way, be responsible for Rick Scott's reign as the Republican governor of Florida?

Murder is horrible, an unsolved murder is worse, and the murder of a police officer in the line of duty creates a reverberation of horror that echoes, in this case, quite literally, through the sands of time. From the balcony of the island's Sliders Seaside Grill, the view of the sand dunes and the blue Atlantic offer an oceanfront experience far different from one that allegedly haunts a murdered deputy sheriff, and his descendants. It is a story, from start to finish, of politics carried to extremes, played out in deadly force near the pristine dunes that would someday become a signature beachfront for a popular restaurant.

It began in Starke, Florida, where Everett E. Johns grew up and married his hometown sweetheart Annie in 1893. They were both young; he was only twenty-four and she was eighteen. The next decade was good to them. Everett was the sheriff of Bradford County, and Everett and Annie had two young sons, Everett and Charley, and a daughter Annie.

Then, in 1904, the good sheriff faced a brutal reelection campaign. The Johns home was set on fire twice. Everett lost the election and, concerned for his family's safety, appealed to a friend for a job in the Nassau County police force. He got the job of deputy sheriff in August of 1905. He moved his family to Fernandina Beach...and he was dead before Christmas.

According to a 1905 issue of *The Telegraph*, a man came to the police station and claimed that his fishing nets were stolen. A warrant was issued

View of the dunes from the balcony at Sliders Seaside Grill.

and Everett, in his horse and buggy, took the man back to the beach and the alleged scene of the crime. In the lonely sand dunes between Fort Clinch and where Sliders now stands, the buggy passenger shot Everett, point blank, through the ear. Everett's body and the murderer's gun were found next to the blood-stained buggy early the next morning. No one was ever arrested for the murder, but people speculated that the deputy was executed to prevent his testimony in an upcoming federal case.

Annie moved back to Starke where she took in boarders to make ends meet, until she eventually remarried, moved to Gainesville, and had three more children. Of the Johns's children, only the youngest, Charley, distinguished himself by entering politics and becoming a renowned member of the infamous Pork Chop Gang.

The Pork Chop gang, so named by *Tampa Tribune* editor James Clendinen, referred to rural Southern lawmakers, all conservative democrats in the 1950s and '60s, who consolidated pork barrel projects for their rich, white friends, while practicing racist policies against the NAACP, and homophobic persecution against scores of professors and students at Florida universities. So reviled was Charley Johns, that his name was eventually removed from a list of distinguished alumni for the University of Florida. One can also speculate that Johns's extreme politics of bigotry and cronyism created a backlash in Florida that ended a century of Democratic influence and ushered in a string of Republican wins culminating in Governor Rick Scott's victory in 2010.

What motivated Charley Johns? Did the violent reelection politics of Bradford County and the consequent unsolved murder of his heroic father ignite his xenophobic fear of anyone and everyone? Or, as a fatherless son, were these traumatic events an indelible influence in his life? Regardless, it's a sad legacy and quite different from the respect awarded his father.

Everett E. Johns is still honored by the Nassau County Police Department as one of its fallen officers killed in the line of duty. In 2006, a twenty-one-gun salute was fired after a solemn ceremony honoring the four officers who lost their lives in the line of duty since 1891. Every year, a top employee of the Nassau County Sheriff's Department is presented with the Deputy Everett E. Johns Distinguished Service Award. The name of Everett E. Johns is inscribed on the National Law Enforcement Memorial in Washington, DC.

According to Amelia Island author Maggie Carter-de Vries, in her book, *Ghosts of Amelia and Other Tales*, "The figure of a man, dressed in old-style garb with a badge on his coat has been seen walking along the beach near Slider's Seaside Grill."

Deputy Everett E. Johns was a protector of the public, and it cost him his life. Perhaps he roams the beach, near the site of his unsolved murder, a fallen officer who refuses to stay down, looking for his family, who he sought to protect and ultimately couldn't.

The History

The name of Slider's Seaside Grill is something of an oxymoron. A "slider" is a small square hamburger sprinkled with onions similar to the kind served at a White Castle or a Krystal's restaurant. But Sliders specializes in seafood and Caribbean food and tries to appeal to families. A small playground is plunked in the sand in view of the servers taking their cigarette breaks. Yet it's a spot with white, sugary dunes and an ocean view of the sunrise. It always has been popular.

Back in 1944, the restaurant was known as The Seaside Inn. It provided rooms as well as food, and the downstairs portion of the hotel still has the original wooden floor, a fireplace, a black-and-white picture of the old joint, and a sign saying The Seaside Inn, which leads to the restrooms. Deeper into World War II, the roadhouse was used as a military detachment headquarters, and, after the war, as a fun-and-sun place for vacationing movie crews. When the Amelia Island Plantation opened in the '70s the restaurant end of the business really picked up. The turn of the twenty-first century wasn't as profitable, and the restaurant closed briefly in 2002. There was a full renovation for its reopening in 2003.

On a weekend night, patrons sit outside at a long table and listen to live rock and roll, surrounded by raucous locals and, perhaps, a rowdy wedding party. Quiet lunches are available on the upper balcony. The tables are wooden shutters with a glass top. The renovated second floor has yellow pine floors, a brand new bar with sparkling glasses and gleaming taps, and floor-to-ceiling windows with a view of the beach.

Aside from Slider's famous fried pickles, their crab cakes, shrimp, and salads are popular favorites. Guests may idly watch a guy on the beach trying to push his car out of the sand while they finish their grouper sandwiches.

There is a certain comfortable invisible boundary between Sliders and the wild and desolate dunes where the wandering spirit of a heroic officer may roam. The contrast is part of the restaurant's charm.

Visitor Information

Sliders Seaside Grill
1998 South Fletcher Avenue
Fernandina Beach, FL 32034
www.slidersseaside.com

Where Everett E. Johns still walks.

Chapter 26

St. Peters Episcopal Church

A man's manners are a mirror in which he shows his portrait.
—Johann Wolfgang von Goethe

The Haunting

Told by Penny Sansbury, volunteer docent for the Amelia Island Museum of The History:

The story I want to tell you is about two of our most prominent citizens: Amelia and Major Duryee. He was a deacon here [St. Peters Episcopal Church], a lumber baron, and he owned some property downtown. He was even involved in local politics. He was also sort of a dandy, very vain about his looks.

Amelia was just a character. She was known for how protective she was of animals. If she saw someone beating horse or a dog, she would just come after him with an umbrella.

She and the Major didn't get along very well. In fact, they didn't like each other much.

Since Major Duryee was sort of a politician, and very vain, he donated a mirror to the church. It was a peer mirror, very expensive, extending from floor to ceiling. He put it where the choir would have to pass, so he could check himself out before he went to sing.

After he died, Amelia moved up north.

Some time after that, around Christmas, the priest who conducted services at the church, was opening up Christmas presents. He opened up a package of cookies, he opened up a package of fruitcake, and then he opened up another package...of ashes. He called up his housekeeper, and asked, "What is this?"

She said, "I thought it was a Christmas present, so I put it under the tree."

He was preparing for Christmas so he wasn't really sure what the ashes were for. Then he got another letter saying these were Amelia Duryee's ashes, and her son was coming down later to plan a memorial service for her. The priest wasn't sure where to keep Amelia's ashes, so he put her remains at the bottom of the peer mirror to keep until after the holiday when he would be ready to deal with them.

He got up the next morning, went into the church, and the peer mirror was cracked from top to bottom.

When the housekeeper saw it, she said, "Huh. I guess he didn't want to spend eternity with her, either."

A former wooden mission, the exterior of St. Peters Episcopal Church, designed by famed architect Robert Sands Schuyler.

The History

Most of the structures in the historic district were built in the post-Civil War era. St. Peters Episcopal Church began quite a bit earlier as a wooden mission in 1858. During the Civil War, it housed federal officers. Like so many wooden structures in the late nineteenth century it burned down in 1892, but it was reconstructed a year later in its present Gothic-revival style by Robert Sands Schuyler, a noted architect of Episcopal churches (he also designed Old St. Andrews Church in downtown Jacksonville).

Schuyler was a union officer and a Civil War hero of the Shenandoah campaign in the battle against Stonewall Jackson. Major George Fairbanks, who fought on the Confederate side in the Civil War, brought Schuyler to Fernandina Beach. The two became best friends and Schuyler designed Fairbanks's home in 1885.

Unfortunately, Schuyler's reconstruction efforts contributed to his demise; he died in 1895 from complications connected to an injury he sustained while overseeing construction on St. Peters Episcopal Church. The masterpiece responsible for his demise is featured on its website as "The Jewel of Centre Street." It typifies many features of Gothic architecture: imbedded windows with narrow arches that come steeply to a point, vertically sloped roof, serrated tower. Twenty-nine of the imbedded windows are stained glass, including memorials, such as the "Holy Innocents triple window" that memorializes thirty-six children who died during a yellow fever epidemic in 1877, and "The Doctors window, "dedicated to the memory of two doctors who came to Fernandina to help with the epidemic and ended up becoming victims themselves. Thick walls made of tabby, an indigenous mixture of oyster shell, lime, and exterior cement, ensure that St. Peters, while not the only church in historic downtown Fernandina Beach by a long shot, is certainly the most ornate.

This is also an active church with three Sunday services, a nursery, a children's chapel, ten "Christian formation" classrooms, a recreational youth center, a parish [Burns] hall, and the cathedral itself. Its antecedent management is prestigious as well. According to an article in the local *News-Leader* by reporter Heather Perry, the diocese, in 2011, promoted the rector of St. Peters, George D. Young III, to Bishop of East Tennessee.

Then there is the large cemetery dating back to the nineteenth century, a pervasive presence behind the church. The cemetery gates are close to where the original wooden missionary first stood, which was a long time ago, but not quite as long a time since the Major's gift to the reconstructed church, a peer mirror, cracked after a night near his contentious wife's cremated ashes.

Consider that ordinary broken mirrors yield seven years bad luck. Consider how many more years of bad luck an immense broken peer mirror generates.

From a side street: St. Peters Episcopal Church at night.

Graveyard behind the church where Amelia and Major Duryee lie side by side for eternity.

Major Duryee has had a long time to endure such a binding superstition.

Despite the ill will between them, the remains of Major and Amelia Duryee lie side by side in an eternal truce, if not at rest, in the cemetery behind St. Peters Episcopal Church.

Visitor Information

St. Peters Episcopal Church
801 Atlantic Avenue
Fernandina Beach, FL 32034
www.stpetersparish.org

Chapter 27

T. J. Eppes House

It's a perfect night for mystery and horror. The air itself is filled with monsters.

—Character of Elsa Lanchester as Mary Shelley
in 1935 film *The Bride of Frankenstein*

The Haunting

Told by Penny Sansbury a volunteer docent for Amelia Island Museum of History:

The great-great-grandson of President Thomas Jefferson and the son of a Monticello judge built this house; his name was Thomas Jefferson Eppes—called T. J.—and he built it for his wife Celeste.

Celeste was this young beauty with long, flowing raven hair. They said she was a Cajun, and she was kind of like a tiny firecracker. She was as colorful on the outside as she was explosive on the inside. And she created quite a stir when she came to Fernandina because she was so flamboyant. She loved to flaunt her beauty.

T. J. was an architect, he was a surveyor, he was a railroad man; in those days, you didn't need degrees to do those things—they were just learned professions. He built this house for Celeste, and then he went out of town quite a bit on business. When he came back, Celeste told him that a man had insulted her, a Major Ferdinand Suhrer [manager of the Mansion House Hotel where the Eppes lived until their house was built].

T. J. was upset that Suhrer had insulted his wife. He went over to the hotel and called him out on the porch. He took his gun, supposedly just to threaten him [Suhrer], but he wound up shooting him in the lung and Suhrer died.

Before he died, Suhrer was lying on the porch of the Mansion Hotel, and he said, "Jeff, what have I done?"

T. J. said, "You've insulted my wife."

"As God as my witness, I've done no such thing," Suhrer said.

This whole thing—T. J. shooting Suhrer—split the town. It was a very emotional event, and it was a small town. People were saying, "Celeste is flamboyant; surely she was asking for it." Suhrer was a family man [he was married with six children]. Other people were saying, "'Well, she was insulted, and a husband should defend his wife's honor."

The former home of a murderer who was also a descendant of President Thomas Jefferson.

There was a trial, it was moved down to St. Johns County. And in the transcript of the trial, Celeste admits that she did make up the story to make her husband jealous. The jury acquitted T. J., because, in those days, he had a justifiable defense.

Celeste haunts this house. She died in childbirth and T. J. married again to a woman named Kate. Kate was standing in the bedroom one day and an apparition appeared at the foot of the bed. She was in a white nightgown and she had long, flowing dark hair.

Kate said, "Celeste is that you?"

The apparition said, "Yes."

"Well, what happened to your beautiful hair?" Kate asked. There was a long, wide white streak in Celeste's ghostly hair.

Celeste said, "It's my mark of shame, my mark of Cain, because I committed murder."

So, her ghost is not malicious in any way, just a presence. We had someone come on the tour one night who grew up around here, and she said, "I went to school with the children who lived in this house. And they all had white streaks in their hair."

We're thinking, "Oh, yeah, pulling our legs here." Then we had a second person tell us that, and a third. So supposedly, the children who grew up in the house had white streaks in their hair.

The History

Built in 1885, the Eppes house fell into disrepair and stood abandoned by the end of the twentieth century. According to column Nassau Neighbors reporter Dickie Anderson, for *The Florida-Times Union*, in a 2001 article titled "Island awash in haunts" the "fading mansion" lacked paint and many of its windows were broken. That changed in November of the same year when a private owner bought the roomy mansion of 3,000-plus square feet for just under $100,000.

Worth more than five times that amount today, the Eppes House has had five owners since then and each has worked to enhance and to restore its natural beauty. Although it is part of the Historic Walking Tour in the Fernandina Beach historic district (also known as the Silk Stocking District because of its well-heeled owners) the Eppes House is not listed on the National Register of Historic Place listings in Nassau County, Florida. Perhaps because of his lack of professional training, Eppes was considered more of a vernacular than a certified architect.

The house is quite beautiful. It features a porch on the second story, bay windows throughout, and dome-shaped glass panels on the front door. Most distinctive is the gingerbread trim fashioned to show the profession of the homeowner. Eppes was a surveyor and the trim displays shapes of a compass and a plummet [a weight, with a honed tip].

According to a local reporter, Ryan Smith—who spent the night in the Eppes House in 2008 hoping for a glimpse of Celeste—the residence is completely modernized with a swimming pool, remodeled kitchen, and cheery yellow walls. Smith notes, however, that the floors are original, and the staircase leading up to Celeste's haunted bedroom is narrow and spooky.

Smith points out, as far as haunted houses go, that the Eppes House is unusual because it is not haunted by the murder victim and the murder itself did not occur anywhere near the house. Major Suhrer, a German immigrant who fought as a Union soldier in the Civil War, lies in Bosque Bello Cemetery located on the edge of the town. Celeste is buried with her stillborn baby in the cemetery behind St. Peters Episcopal Church on Atlanta Avenue.

Nevertheless, according to local lore, a shadow of her former vivacious self still lingers in the Eppes House consumed with guilt and infamy. One can argue that her hotheaded husband, T.J., is the one at fault for allowing masculine pride to lead to murder. Instead, Celeste withstands the worst of the horror of Suhrer's murder. Yet all she wanted was a little attention from her husband.

Like the Bride of Frankenstein, she discovered she was married to a monster. The shock has streaked her hair with white.

Visitor Information

T. J. Eppes House
31 South 10th Street
Fernandina Beach, FL 32034

Chapter 28

The Old School House

The Helicon of too many poets is not a hill crowned with sunshine and visited by the Muses and the Graces, but an old, moldering house, full of gloom and haunted by ghosts.

—Henry Wadsworth Longfellow

The Haunting

Told by Steve Sansbury, volunteer docent for The Amelia Island Museum of History:

This old building functioned as a schoolhouse, and, at one point, someone noticed a leak in the roof. They had to wait until it rained to figure out where the leak was. Then they sent a workman in to look for the leak.

He had to climb up on some scaffolding. What they think happened was he made a misstep; he fell off the scaffolding all the way down to the floor. He was severely injured, he climbed back up on the edge of this window, and he banged on the window. However, it was raining; there was no one in the street. No one came. So he died. He was found bloody, dead, and lying in a corner. There was a bloody handprint on the window.

After that, children would tell their teacher, "There's a man lying out in the hall." The teacher would come out in the hall, and there would be no man. And the story that is told is that when it rains, you can see bloody handprints on the window. They cleaned the handprints off, but every time it rains, they come back.

Now as a side note, a couple of years ago there was a woman here on the tour who was in charge of the company who inspects these buildings. And she said she never liked to go up to the second floor, she always took someone with her because she didn't like to go by herself. She didn't know why, it just gave her the willies. Now she knows why, but she still won't go up on the second floor by herself.

The Old School House on Centre Street that features bloody handprints on the windows when it rains.

The History

According to 2012 estimates, the Nassau County property appraiser lists the dimensions of the old schoolhouse at close to 8,000 square feet and its worth at half a million dollars. The late nineteenth century structure is yet another beautiful building designed by Robert S. Schuyler, and, like so many reputedly haunted "places," it is an integral part of Fernandina Beach's historic district.

Functioning as the old Fernandina High School until at least 1924, it was also the site of a class reunion for its ten graduates (nine girls, one boy) in 1974. Their class motto was, "Life is a picture, paint it well." The picture of educational establishments in Fernandina Beach changed, of course, to a more elaborate structure accommodating almost 900 students.

Thus, the old schoolhouse has housed office space for many years. An oak tree draped with Spanish moss shelters the old two-story brick and mortar building on Atlantic Avenue, which bears the legend of District School No. 1 1886. The building seems less a structure than an accumulation of its notable parts; even the sidewalk leading up to the old schoolhouse maintains the original octagonal pavers.

According to docent Sansbury, the green-trimmed frames where bloody handprints appear in inclement weather once encased the original ripple glass [sheet of textured glass with marked surface waves] in the windows, since silica glass didn't emerge until the twentieth century. The steps where students used to tread are made of brick and slate, leading up to a door painted green. Clearly, an affluent community commissioned the old schoolhouse.

At night, though, the old school house looms, a dark and silent hull on the far end of the historic district. If the old Fernandina High School's class of '24 regaled their motto of life as a blank canvas, requiring the skillful artistry of a life well lived...well, there's also a story behind every picture and shades of somber and garish hues as well as light.

In the case of the Old Schoolhouse, add a bloody embellishment to the picture; the streak of red fingerprints on rain splattered glass.

Visitor Information

Old School House
914 Atlantic Avenue
Fernandina Beach, FL 32034

BAKER COUNTY

Chapter 29

Olustee Battlefield Historic State Park

Olustee's woods are silent now, the battle smoke has fled...

—Benjamin R. Gormley
Written for the 125th anniversary of the Battle of Olustee

The Haunting

Olustee, the famous Civil War battlefield in Baker County, has its share of ghost stories. People who camp nearby claim they can still hear the sounds of battle whistling in the wind: the shrieks of horses, the cries of men, artillery, cannon fire. There are the reports of orbs and apparitions. Yet aside from these sketchy speculations of specters, there is actual historic documentation of a ghost. The ghost story concerns a Union soldier, Private John Rowley, who was haunted by a fellow soldier, Private Jerome Dupoy, in the aftermath of the Olustee battle. The haunting resulted in Rowley being charged and then executed for treason.

Both men were members of the Seventh Connecticut Infantry Regiment, Company D. There was bad blood between Rowley and Dupoy that culminated in a fight with knives. Dupoy won the fight, and Rowley was left bleeding with gashes from Dupoy's knife. Other soldiers claimed to hear Rowley promising revenge.

In February 1864, during the battle of Olustee, Dupoy suffered a fatal bullet shot right through his head. Initially, no one suspected Rowley, but gradually the rumors became rampant. Eventually, Rowley was arrested and confined to the guardhouse.

The matter may have ended there, but Rowley complained constantly that he could not sleep. In fact, he claimed to see ghosts. Soon the whole story came out. Rowley had deliberately killed Dupoy. Rowley's confession was published in May of 1864 in the Danbury, Connecticut, newspaper, *The Jeffersonian*:

Olustee Battlefield Monument and portable cannon.

> *Since the battle, I have dreaded nights, for they are horrible nights. When on picket duty I always see Dupoy stand a little away in front, his face full of blood and the bullet hole in his forehead. At night in my dreams, he stands at the entrance, I awake. He is there, pale and bloody, but vanishes as soon as I see him. I could not keep the horrible crime a secret any longer.*

Rowley was court-martialed, found guilty, and hung in September of 1864, just seven months before Lee surrendered to Grant and ended the Civil War.

The war between Rowley and Dupoy continues to play out, at least in memory, on the Olustee battlefield.

The History

The actual battle of Olustee between Union and Confederate forces took place in February, and there are reports of bitter cold and soldiers breaking ice on the rim of their canteens. But the battlefield is hot as blazes in the spring and in the summer. It is eerily quiet, too. There are no sounds, even of birds, and traffic on nearby US 90 is scarce. Olustee is a one-traffic-light town, and aside from the battlefield, there is not much to see except for an out-of-gas Citgo station offering cold beer and deep fried gizzards.

Part of the Osceola National Forest, Olustee battlefield contains almost 700 acres of open pinewoods, some of it blackened and scorched from recent fires. There are also some picnic benches, a few monuments, battlefield trails, cannons, a ranger tower, a museum, and a cemetery near the railroad tracks where a cross marks the mass burial of 200 Union soldiers. It is also home to some wildlife, including the sand hill crane, woodpeckers, scrub jays, and gopher tortoises. Yet, no one really comes to Olustee for the nature. They come for the history and the reenactments.

Every February, close to the date of the Civil War battle and the long President's Day weekend, hundreds of Union and Confederate reenactors converge for the annual Olustee Festival, which fetes thousands of visitors. There are craft shows, a band, food, and fun runs, but the main event is the historical reenactment of the only major Civil War battle that took place in Florida. And the Confederates won it. Year after year, they win it again.

The story of the Battle of Olustee goes back to an election year, 1864, when Abraham Lincoln was trying to shore up his chances for another presidential term. Although Florida was one of the first states to secede from the Union in 1861, Lincoln and his advisors knew that local sentiment for the war was divided between Union and Confederate sympathies. In retrospect, they clearly overestimated the momentum of Union support, as they proceeded with their plan to establish Jacksonville as a Union bastion, and stop the flow of food, salt, and cattle from Florida to the rest of the Confederate

Scorched pines framing the battlefield trail of Olustee.

nation. They also wanted to restore Florida to the Union and clinch Lincoln's chances for reelection.

Alas, for the best laid plans. Union General Truman Seymour marched from South Carolina to Jacksonville with 5,500 men; these included the famous 54th Massachusetts infantry of black soldiers recruited by abolitionists and led by Colonel Robert Shaw. Seymour easily took over Jacksonville and proceeded along Lake City west of the St. Johns River. Confederates would brawl with Union soldiers and then retreat, drawing the Union army toward Olustee where Confederate General Joseph Finegan had, with the help of General Beauregard, amassed 5,000 soldiers mostly from Charleston and Savannah.

The outcome on February 20th was a close confrontation on the Olustee battlefield; soldiers claimed they could see the inscriptions on the belt buckles of their opponents. It lasted four hours, until Union resistance disintegrated and they retreated to Jacksonville. The 54th Massachusetts Infantry distinguished themselves in battle, serving as the rearguard of the retreating army, possibly

Live reenactment of the Battle of Ocean Pond.

saving it from complete destruction. They also performed the astounding feat of hand pulling a train of wounded Union soldiers for five miles down a railroad track. They did all of this for seven dollars a month, when the army remembered to pay them, which it seldom did. Although the 54th lost only eighty-six men in the actual battle, their overall casualties turned out to be much higher. Confederate president Jefferson Davis declared that any black man serving in the Union Army, and any white man commanding him, must be executed on the spot. So the black wounded soldiers left behind on the battlefield were murdered by roving bands of Confederate soldiers.

Overall, Union casualties were high: 1,861 men killed, wounded, or missing. It was a stunning victory for the south and for Florida in particular. And Confederate forces may have changed the course of the Civil War if they had followed Seymour and annihilated what was left of his troops. But they didn't pursue the Union men until the next day, and by then, the army was reestablished in Jacksonville. Florida was once again delegated to the peripheries of US military operations and its internal hostilities, skirmishes, and raids.

Tourists can follow the battlefield trail, read the information kiosks, and swelter in the heat of a typical Florida day. At the museum, a tape of banjo music plays "Dixie," and a continuous video of *The Battle of Ocean Pond* displays on a small screen. Visitors may meet people like Steve Lynch of Boston whose great-grandfather, Jeremiah Hogan, was a Union veteran of the Olustee battlefield. He joined the army at the age of fifteen and was a member of the 3rd Rhode Island Infantry, Company C. He took a bullet in his leg at Olustee and limped for the rest of his life.

Flag experts congregate in Olustee as well. They may point out that the popular Confederate flag, often displayed as a decal on pickups with gun racks, the one with the star-spangled cross, is in fact, the Confederate naval flag and not the one carried into battle. To prove their point they may gesture to the Confederate flag mounted behind glass in the museum viewing room, which looks a lot like the Union flag only with fewer stars and stripes, as it represents seceded states. But it's mounted upside down. The star points to hell instead of heaven, and the red bar is supposed to be at the bottom. Whether mounting the Confederate flag incorrectly was a mistake or a statement by the state of Florida, one can only speculate.

Regardless, the bloody history of the Olustee battlefield scars the pristine landscape, and it's a scar that is reopened and reexamined annually in a simulated version of a battle that occurred almost 150 years ago. Then the ghosts of Finegan, Seymour, and Shaw reemerge, as does the 54th Massachusetts infantry and countless other desperate men. Including Rowley and Dupoy.

Even though they are all only memories.

And long dead.

Visitor Information

Olustee Battlefield Historic State Park
5890 Battlefield Trail Road
Olustee, FL 32087
www.floridastateparks.org/olusteebattlefield/
http://battleofolustee.org/

CONCLUSION

Shakespeare famously said, "What's past is prologue." We would contend that the past is also a portrait. Bob and I hope that we've painted a picture of northeast Florida's past that honors the language of the land and the lives of its inhabitants. It's a picture painted in landscapes, on terraces, in small rooms, and from sweeping staircases. Like all Floridians, in recording its history, we've become part of it. And, you, faithful reader, have joined us in its rarified territory. We hope to meet again, perhaps in another part of the peninsula. *Women in White*, and the land they haunt, have many more stories to tell.

Bibliography

Books, Magazine Articles, Journal Articles, Websites

90 Years of Service, 1873-1963; the Story of St. Luke's Hospital. Jacksonville: American Hospital Association Resource Center, 1963. Center for Hospital and Healthcare Administration History.

Armstrong, Wayne P. "The Life & Loves of Sand Dunes." *Exploring the Southwest Desert.* DesertUSA.com, 1998. 12 May 2012. www.desertusa.com/magjan98/dunes/jan_dune1.html.

The Battle of Ocean Pond. US Military Historic Institute. Videocassette.

Belleville, Bill. *River of Lakes: A Journey on Florida's St. Johns River.* Athens: University of Georgia Press, 2000.

Belleville, Bill. *Salvaging the Real Florida: Lost and Found in the State of Dreams.* Gainesville: University Press of Florida, 2011.

Benington, Dale K. "Yellow Bluff Fort Dedicated to the Memory of the Confederate Soldiers Who Defended Jacksonville." *The Historical Marker Database.* 23 July 2010. 7 Jan. 2012. www.hmdb.org/marker.asp?marker=33458.

Birdwell, April F. "Kingsley Plantation: A Legacy Revealed." *Florida* Fall 2007.

Braukman, Stacy Lorraine. *Communists and Perverts under the Palms: The Johns Committee in Florida, 1956-1965.* Gainesville: University Press of Florida, 2012.

Bronson, Bertrand Harris. *The Ballad as Song.* Berkeley: University of California, 1969.

Burt, Al. *Becalmed in the Mullet Latitudes: Al Burt's Florida.* Port Salerno, FL: Florida Classics Library, 1983.

Carlson, Charlie. *Weird Florida: Your Travel Guide to Florida's Local Legends and Best Kept Secrets.* New York, NY: Barnes & Nobles, 2005.

Carter-de, Vries Maggie. *Ghosts of Amelia & Other Tales.* Bloomington, IN: AuthorHouse, 2008.

"Cemetery Section Map—Amelia Island and Nassau County Florida Cemeteries." *Old Bosque Bello Index Map. Cemetery Section Map—Amelia Island and Nassau County Florida Cemeteries.* 21 Jan. 2012. www.aigensoc.org/cemeterySectionMap.asp?cid=1066.

"Clay County Historical Archives: Ghosts." *Clay County Historical Archives: Ghosts.* 6 June 2012. http://archives.clayclerk.com/ghosts.html.

Cohen, Myer M. *Notices of Florida and The Campaigns.* New York: Charleston, S.C. Burges & Honour, 1836.

Congdon, Kristin G., and Tina Bucuvalas. *Just above the Water: Florida Folk Art.* Jackson: University of Mississippi, 2006.

Connerly, Charles E. "From Racial Zoning to Community Empowerment: The Interstate Highway System and the African American Community in Birmingham Alabama." *Journal of Planning, Education and Research* (2009).

Corley, Lyn. "Battle for America." 2 June 2012. http://stonecutwithouthands.com/battle_for_america2.pdf.

Cornelison, Tom. "Close Encounters." *Jacksonville Magazine* Feb. 2011: 38-39.
Cornelison, Tom. "Family Affairs." *Jacksonville Magazine* Jan. 2012: 30-31.
Cowart, John W. "Yellow Jack in Jacksonville: The 1888 Epidemic." 2005. 4 Feb. 2012. www.cowart.info/Florida%20History/YellowJack/YellowJack.htm.
Cox, Dale. "Defender of the St. Johns River." *ExploreSouthernHistory.com*.
Yellow Bluff Fort Historic State Park, 2011. 7 Jan. 2012. www.exploresouthernhistory.com/yellowbluffort.html.
"Dames Point/Crosses Point." *Florida History Online*. University of North Florida. 5 Mar. 2012. www.unf.edu/floridahistoryonlin/Plantations/plantations/Dames_Point-Crosses_Point.htm.
Davis, Jerold H. "Seventh Connecticut Infantry Regiment." *Battle of Olustee*. 3 May 2012. http://battleofolustee.org/7th_ct_inf.html.
De, Quesada A. M. *A History of Florida Forts: Florida's Lonely Outposts*. Charleston, SC: History Press, 2006.
DiRienzo, Patty. *Florida: A Journey through Its Colorful past*. Boulder, CO: Westcliffe Pub. 2008.
Douglas, Marjorie S. *The Everglades: River of Grass*. Miami: Banyan, 1978.
Dyckman, Martin A. *Reubin O'D. Askew and the Golden Age of Florida Politics*. Gainesville: University Press of Florida, 2011.
Fairlie, Margaret C. "The Yellow Fever Epidemic of 1888 in Jacksonville." *The Florida Historical Quarterly* 19.2 (1940): 95-108.
Fichter, George S., and George Cardin. *Floridians All*. Gretna: Pelican Pub. Co. 1991.
"Fifty-fourth Massachusetts Infantry." *The Battle of Olustee*. 3 June 2012. http://battle of olustee.org/54th_mass_inf.html.
Florida: A Guide to the Southernmost State. New York: Oxford Univ. Pr. 1956.
"Fold Heritage Awards Recipient: Ray Singleton." *Florida Folk Life Programs*. 3 Mar. 2012. www.flheritage.com/preservation/folklife/awards/awardDetails.cfm?id=82.
Freethinker. London: G.W. Foote &, 1881.
Gannon, Michael. *Rebel Bishop: Augustin Verot, Florida's Civil War Prelate*. Gainesville, FL: University Press of Florida, 1997.
Garrison, B. *More Civil War Curiosities*. Nashville: Rutledge Hill, 1995.
Godwin, Carmen. "A Town Called Franklin Town." *Amelia Island Magazine* Aug. 2003: 13-14.
Gonzalez, Louis. "The Poltergeist Phenomenon." *Globat Login*. 7 Jan. 2012. www.scspr.org/articles/poltergeist.htm.
Hardee, Suzanne Davis., and Sara Dudney. *The Golden Age of Amelia Island: Booklet II: The Churches*. Fernandina Beach, FL: Amelia Island Museum of History, 1994.
Haskins, Lola. *Fifteen Florida Cemeteries: Strange Tales Unearthed*. Gainesville: University of Florida, 2011.
Hauck, Dennis William. *The National Directory of Haunted Places*. Sacramento, CA: Athanor, 1994.
"History Lives in City's Old House." *The Ind. Traveler* 23 May 1979: 9.
"A History of the Casa Marina Hotel." *Jax Islander Magazine* 2011.
Huffman, Alan. "An American Beach." *The Magazine of the Historic Trust for National Preservation* (2005). *The Magazine for the Historic Trust for National Preservation*. July-Aug. 2005. 4 Mar. 2011. www.preservationnation.org/magazine/2005/july-august/an-american-beach.htm
Huffstodt, Jim. "Napoleon Bonaparte Broward: Gun Runner, Riverboat Captain, People's Champion...and Florida Governor." *Tallahassee Magazine* Jan.-Feb. 2010.
Hunt, Bruce. *Visiting Small-town Florida*. Sarasota, FL: Pineapple Press, 1997.
Jenkins, Greg. *Florida's Ghostly Legends and Haunted Folklore*. Vol. 2. Sarasota:

Pineapple Press, 2005.
Johannes, Jan H., and Lynne L. Johannes. *Yesterday's Reflections II, Nassau County, Florida: A Pictorial History*. Fernandina Beach, FL: Lexington Ventures, 2000.
Jung, Emma, Marie-Louise Von. Franz, and Andrea Dykes. *The Grail Legend*. Princeton (New Jersey): Princeton UP, 1998.
Kallina, Edmund F. *Claude Kirk and the Politics of Confrontation*. Gainesville: University Press of Florida, 1993.
Kornwolf, James D. and Georgiana Wallis. Kornwolf. *Architecture and Town Planning in Colonial North America*. Baltimore: Johns Hopkins UP, 2002.
Landers, Jane. *Colonial Plantations and Economy in Florida*. Gainesville: University Press of Florida, 2000.
Lapham, Dave. *Ghosthunting Florida*. Cincinnati, OH: Clerisy, 2010.
Lawson, W.B. "Christmas Cheer: Florida House Inn Reopens in Fernandina Beach." *Amelia Island Travel News* 02 Dec. 2010.
Lawson, W.B. "R.I.P.: Bosque Bello Cemetery, Fernandina Beach." *Amelia Island Perspective, Amelia Island Travel News* 30 Oct. 2009.
Litrico, Charles. "The Eppes House." *Amelia Now* Spring 2004.
Mabry, Donald. "Florida's Napoleon." The Historical Text Archive, 1990-2011. 3 Mar. 2012. http://historicaltextarchive.com/sections.php?action=read$artid=771.
Mack, Patricia. "Everything's Better with a Beach View." *Casa Marina Jacksonville Beach Florida Hotel Review*. 23 Nov. 2011. 1 Feb. 2012. www.gayot.com/travel/hotels/casa-marina-jacksonville-beach-florida.html.
Martin, C. Lee. *Florida Ghosts and Pirates: Jacksonville, Fernandina, Amelia Island, St. Augustine, Daytona*. Atglen, PA: Schiffer Pub. 2008.
McGoldrick, Joseph Thomas, Sister. *Beyond the Call: The Legacy of the Sisters of St. Joseph of St. Augustine, Florida*. Xlibris, 2007.
Merritt, Ster. "A Century of Medicine in Jacksonville and Duval County." *Saints & Angels*. University of Florida Press, 1949. 8 Feb. 2012. www.catholic.org/saints/saint.php?saint_id=76.
Moore, Roger. *Amelia Island and Fernandina Beach*. Amelia Island, FL: Photographs Naturally, 2001.
"New Berlin Cemetery." *USGen Archives*. Ed. Jan Smith and Betty Bleshoy. 17 Feb. 2012. http://files.usgwarchives.net/fl/duval/cemetery/newberlin.txt.
Nolan, David. *Fifty Feet in Paradise: The Booming of Florida*. San Diego: Harcourt Brace Jovanovich, 1984.
O'Dell, Carol. "A Fernandina Ghost Tale." *Amelia Islander Magazine* Jan.–Feb. 2012: 36.
"Once Upon a Time...A Princess Lived." 7 Jan. 2012. www.flaglerlibraryfriend.com/flaglerhistory/princess/princess.htm.
"A Physician's Last Act." *Florida Medical Magazine* Winter 2010. www.mydigitalpublication.com/display_article.php?id=322370
Powell, Jack. *Haunting Sunshine*. Sarasota, FL: Pineapple Press, 2001.
Proctor, Samuel. "Napoleon B. Broward." *The Florida Historical Quarterly* 26.2 (1947): 1.
Proctor, Samuel. *Napoleon Bonaparte Broward: Florida's Fighting Democrat*. Gainesville: University Press of Florida, 1993.
Puterbaugh, Parke, and Alan Bisbort. *Moon Florida Beaches: The Best Places to Swim, Play, Eat, and Stay*. Emeryville, CA: Avalon Travel, 2006.
Raser, William. "And the Rest Is History." *Amelia Islander Magazine* 2000.
Schafer, Daniel L. *Thunder on the River: The Civil War in Northeast Florida*. Gainesville: University Press of Florida, 2010.
Singer, Steven D. *Shipwrecks of Florida*. Sarasota, FL: Pineapple, 1992.
Straight, William M. "The Yellow Jack." *Journal of the Fl. Medical Association* (1971).
Swanton, John Reed. *Early History of the Creek Indians and Their Neighbors*. Washington: G.P.O., 1922.

Sweet, Frank W. *The Invasion of Spanish Florida*. Palm Coast, FL: Backintyme, 2000.

Travel Guide to Florida's Local Legends and Best Kept Secrets. New York: Sterling, 2005.

US Department of the Interior Ecological and Historic Preserve. "Yellow Bluff." *Experience Your America*. 7 Jan. 2012. www.nps.gov/timu/planyourvisit/upload/civil_war_site_bulletin.pdf.

US Florida State Parks. National Park Service. *Timucuan Ecological and Historical Preserve*. Fort George Island State Cultural Park, 27 Aug. 2005. 4 Jan. 2012. www.nps.gov/timu/historyculture/upload/saturiwa_trail_text.pdf.

Walch, Barbara H. *Frank B. Butler: Lincolnville Businessman and Founder of St. Augustine, Florida's Historic Black Beach*. St. Augustine: R.B. Hadley Sr., 1992.

Wilbanks, William. *Forgotten Heroes: Police Officers Killed in Early Florida, 1840–1925*. Paducah, KY: Turner, 1998.

Willingham, Ben H. and Jeffrey L. Sizemore, eds. *Florida in Turmoil, 'The Terrible War Years 1861-1865*. Jacksonville: Museum of Southern History, 2011.

Winter, Nevin O. *Florida, the Land of Enchantment*. The Page Company, 1918.

Wood, Wayne W., Carole L. Fader, and Emily Retherford. Lisska. *Jacksonville Family Album: 150 Years of the Art of Photography*. Jacksonville, FL: Jacksonville Historical Society, 2005.

"Yellow Bluff Fort Site Photos." *Yellow Bluff Fort Site Photos*. 21 June 2012. www.civilwaralbum.com/misc17/yellowbluff1.htm.

Newspapers, Documents, Interviews

Adams, Charles S., ed. *Report of the Jacksonville Auxiliary Sanitary Association of Jacksonville, Florida. Covering the Work of the Association during the Yellow Fever Epidemic, 1888*. Rep. Library of the University of California, Los Angeles. Published under the Supervision of the Executive Committee of the Association.

"American Beach Property Owner's Association." *2012 Historic American Beach* (Spring 2012).

Anderson, Dickie. "Island Awash in Haunts." *Florida Times-Union* [Jacksonville] Oct. 2001.

Avantevilla at Jacksonville Beach, Inc. v. Candyce Breidert, as Personal Representative of the Estate of Darlene E. Payson. In the District Court of Appeal First District, State of Florida Case No. 1D06-4880.

Avery, Stephen. "Side Lined Restaurateur Passed Time with Model Boats." *The Jacksonville Beaches,* 24 May 1989.

Barbee, J.E. "A TPC (tournament Player's Championship) Food Tradition." *Florida Times-Union* [Jacksonville] 1993.

Belcher, Harold J. *Franklintown Cemetery*. Mar. 1992. Records. The General Duncan Lamont Clinch Historical Society of Amelia Island, Fernandina Beach.

Bland and Associates, Inc. *Historic Content and References from the Historic Properties,* Resurvey. Nassau County Florida, Fernandina Beach. 2007: 41.

Burmeister, Carol. "Preserving Mayport's Earliest History." *Florida Times-Union* [Jacksonville] 5 Aug. 2000

Curtain, Cara. "Bosque Bello Cemetery-City Sidebar." *News-Leader* [Fernandina Beach] Nov. 2002.

Davis, George T. "Notes from Meeting." Amelia Island Fernandina Restoration Foundation. Fernandina Beach. 24 Nov. 1992.

Duval County Property Appraisers Office, 1712 Beach. 11 Feb. 2011. Raw data. Official Records, Jacksonville Beach.

"Ex-Governor Broward Is Dead and Floridians Mourn." *The Evening Independent* [St. Petersburg] 1 Oct. 1910.

FitzRoy, Maggie. "If There's a Ghost at Ginger's Place, It's Not the Only One at the Beaches." *Florida Times-Union* [Jacksonville] 19 Aug. 2010.

Flagler County Tourist Development Council. *Flagler County's Princess Place Preserve.* Bureau of Historical Museums, 2011.

Flaisig, Liz. "1870's Nuns Home Restored." *News-Leader* [Fernandina Beach] 23 June 1999, Homes sec.

Florida Anthropological Society, Inc. Florida Bureau of Archaeological Research. *Florida's Unmarked Burial Law 872.05 Florida Statutes.* Gainesville: Florida Anthropological Society, Florida Bureau of Archaeological Research.

Florida Division of Recreation and Parks. *Yellow Bluff Historic State Park.* Florida Division of Recreation and Parks, 2012.

Florida Master Site File Inventory Forms for 103 S. 9th St. 30 Sept. 1985. Amelia Island Williams House, Historic District. Fernandina Beach, Florida.

Franklin, Marcus. "History on the Sand." *St. Petersburg Times* 2 Aug. 2004.

Fretwall, Jacqueline K., ed. *Kingsley Beatty Gibbs and His Journal of 1840-1843,* 1984. St. Augustine Historical Society: 4-15

Fuller, Barbara. *The Cemeteries of Amelia Island.* 1997. Amelia Island Genealogical Society. Amelia Island Museum of History, Fernandina Beach.

General Duncan Lamont Clinch Family Papers. University of Florida, UF Digital Collections: Letters to General Clinch. 1836-1844 Box 1.

Haddock, Greg. Nassau County Property Appraiser, 614 Ash. 26 Feb. 2007. Raw data. Fernandina Beach.

Hardee, Suzanne. "Bishop Verot and the St. Joseph Nuns." Catholic Women's Group. St. Joseph's Hall. 9 Mar. 1998. Lecture.

Hart, Amelia A. "Nassau ecognizes Officers Who Lost Their Lives." *Florida Times-Union* [Jacksonville] 20 May 2006, Nassau Neighbors sec.

Hines, Jackie. "Marcellus Wiliams." Letter to *Amelia Now Magazine.* 7 Oct. 1994. MS. Amelia Island Museum of History, Fernandina Beach, Florida.

Irish, Tiffani. "Florida Theatre." Personal interview. 6 Jan. 2012.

Jacksonville, Where Florida Begins, North CPAC (North Citizens Planning Advisory Committee) Summary. 14 Dec. 2011. Meeting Summary. FSCJ North Campus, Jacksonville.

Joyce, Sterling. "Casa Marina Hotel." Personal interview. 4 Jan. 2012.

Kevin, Turner. "Amelia Island's Florida House Inn Closes, Continuously in Operation since 1857." *Florida-Times Union* [Jacksonville] 18 Jan. 2010.

Martin, Kimberly N. "Ghost Town." *Folio Weekly* [Jacksonville] Aug. 1998: 14-21.

Mattick, Barbara E. *Ministries in Black and White: The Catholic Sisters of St. Augustine, Florida, 1859-1920, Pg 121.* Diss. Florida State University, 2008. 2008.

Nassau County Property Appraiser, 28 South 7th. 4 Jan. 2011. Raw data. Fernandina Beach.

Nassau County Property Appraiser, 31 S. 10th. 31 Mar. 2012. Raw data. Fernandina Beach.

"Nassau County Sheriff's Office Honors Fallen." *Florida Times-Union* [Jacksonville] 27 May 2010, Special to the Nassau sec.

"N.B. Broward One of Nation's Great Men." *Miami Metropolis* 1910.

Nixon, William G. *Amelia Island Plantation: The First Ten Years.* 1984. The Amelia Island Community Association, 4-11. Arrington Gale, The Amelia Island Museum of History, Fernandina Beach.

O'Brien, Kathleen. "St. Michael Academy Celebrates Legacy." *News-Leader* [Fernandina Beach] 30 Jan. 2008.

Official Records. *Franklintown Cemetery Warranty Deed.* Oct. 1990. Drummond, Morris W. Nassau County Clerk of Circuit Courts, Fernandina Beach.

O'Malley, Brian P. "Recently Discovered Slave Graves Resurrect Discussion on the Origins of African Americans." *Folio Weekly* [Jacksonville] Pgs 3-9 Jan. 2012, Vol. 25, No. 40 ed., Backpage Editorial sec.

"Palace's Fire Erased the Faces of Regulars." *Florida Times-Union* [Jacksonville] 21 Feb. 1999.
"Payson, Darlene." *Florida Times-Union* [Jacksonville] 15 Sept. 2003.
Perry, Heather A. "From Rector Here to Bishop There." *News-Leader* [Fernandina Beach] Feb. 2011.
Perry, Heather A. "Windows Glow in St. Peter's." *News-Leader* [Fernandina] 5 Mar. 2009.
Price, Benjamin. "New Stones Mark Graves of Union Pair at Bosque Bello." *News-Leader* [Fernandina Beach] 29 Dec. 2006.
Rogers, Jonathan. "Singleton's Seafood Shack Stands the Test of Time, Tides." *Florida Times-Union* [Jacksonville] 6 Aug. 1993.
Sansbury, Steve, and Penny Sansbury. "Amelia Island Ghost Tour." Amelia Island Museum of History. Historic District, Fernandina Beach. 9 Jan. 2012. Tour.
Schultz, Cathy. "Book Loft." Personal interview. 15 Oct. 2011.
Smith, Ryan. "All the Makings for a Ghost Story." *News-Leader* [Fernandina Beach] 29 Oct. 2008: 1-6a.
Steere, Elaine. "Class of '24 Comes Home." *News-Leader* [Fernandina Beach] 1974.
Steere, Elaine. "Welcome Back Class of '24." *News-Leader* [Fernandina Beach] 1974.
Thursby, Erin. "Ghosts in the First Coast." *EU Newspaper* [Jacksonville] 25-31 Oct. 2007.
Thurwachter, Mary. "Amelia Island's Williams House." *Palm Beach Post* Feb. 2005.
Trinidad, Alison. "Store Founder Ralph Palmisano Dies." *Florida Times-Union* [Jacksonville] 3 May 2003, Nassau Neighbors ed.
United States. Department of the Interior. National Parks Service. *American Buildings Survey, Florida House*. By Phillip A. Werndli. Washington DC: Written Historical Documentation, 1974. Print. No. Fl-356.
Wadsworth, Gail. "Princess Place Preserve." Personal interview. 17 Oct. 2011.
Weitz, Seth A. *College of Arts and Sciences: Bourbon, Pork Chops, and Red Peppers: Political Immorality in Florida, 1945-1968, Pg 9*. Diss. Department of History, Florida State University, 2007.
Wilbanks, Lynn. "Kingsley Plantation." Personal interview. 16 Oct. 2011.
Wooten, Becky. "Renovate Completed." *Florida Times-Union* [Jacksonville] 6 Mar. 1977.
"Yellow Fever, Description of the Plague at Fernandina. How the Priests and Sisters Devoted Themselves to the Noble Work of Ministering to the Stricken." *Catholic Mirror* 1877, Special Report sec.
Youngblood, Alice P. *African American History, Bosque Bello Cemetery Pg 22, Franklintown Pg 158*. 3 May 1937. Nassau County Federal Writer's Project. Amelia Island Museum of History, Fernandina Beach.
Youngblood, Alice P. *Bosque Bello Cemetery, History Of Fernandina*. 2 Apr. 1937. Nassau County Federal Writer's Project. Amelia Island Museum of History, Fernandina Beach.
Yousefzadeh, Nicole. "Copper Top Restaurant." Personal interview. 6 Jan. 2012.

INDEX